SERVING-ICE-CREAM.COM'S

CLASSIC COLLECTION OF ICE CREAM RECIPES

CONTENTS

SERVING-ICE-CREAM.COM'S

CLASSIC COLLECTION OF ICE CREAM RECIPES

You are about to embark on an exciting ice cream adventure brought to you by one of the web's most popular ice cream websites.

This collection of recipes is considered the "classic" collection. It's a combination of some of the most sought after ice cream recipe flavors...and they're all bundled up for you here in this book.

Before we started making our own ice cream, we were always awestruck whenever we heard of people making their very own ice cream. We thought that creating one's own ice cream from scratch must be the mark of a very talented chef! After all, when you place ice cream in the freezer it's not really supposed to freeze – it's supposed to stay soft and creamy. Surely, making ice cream is a science only the elite could accomplish!

Then, one day we got up the courage to try making our own ice cream. After all, ice cream is our all-time favorite dessert. We didn't expect great success... I'm not even sure we expected ice cream to come out!

We mixed up a batch, threw it in the ice cream maker...and waited. To our surprise, out came ice cream! And it was good! We were hooked! No more store-bought frozen treats for us!

Now it's your turn! May your ice cream adventure begin! We hope you enjoy every batch!

About our homemade ice cream recipes:

- These recipes can be **made with or without an ice cream maker**.
- These recipes make about **1 - 1.5 quarts** of ice cream. Adjust the recipe if you want to make more or less.
- Philadelphia style recipes (recipes that **do not contain eggs**) and Custard style recipes (recipes that **do contain eggs**) are both included for each flavor where applicable.
- Without sacrificing taste or texture, the **sugar and fat have been reduced** in the Philadelphia Style recipes. Feel free to add extra sugar or use milk with more fat, if you prefer.

NO ICE CREAM MAKER?

Making ice cream without an ice cream maker is not difficult. It just takes longer.

Step by Step Instructions
- **Mix up the ice cream recipe as directed.**

Any of the recipes in this book should work just fine. When the recipe tells you to pour the ice cream mixture into the ice cream maker, come back here and follow these simple steps.
- **Pour the ice cream mixture into a wide, airtight container.**

Metal bowls work best (stainless steel is my personal favorite). Ice cream has a smoother consistency when it is frozen faster. Metal bowls speed up the freezing process. If you don't have a metal bowl, plastic will work as well. Make sure the bowl you choose is wide rather than tall. A wide bowl speeds freezing and allows you to mix your ice cream easily.
- **Place ice cream in refrigerator for at least 1 hour.**

Ice cream will need to be in fridge longer if the mixture has been heated and cooked. Ice cream must be well chilled before proceeding.
- **Place the chilled ice cream mixture in the freezer for 30 minutes.**
- **Beat ice cream mixture with an electric mixer until smooth.**

The edges of your ice cream should have started to thicken. Scrape the edges with a fork or spatula and beat with an electric mixer to add air to the mixture and break up ice crystals.

You can use a fork instead of an electric mixer, but the ice cream will be less smooth and creamy.
- **Place ice cream in the freezer for 40 minutes - then beat with an electric mixer.**
- **Repeat "40 minute freeze-then-beat cycle" 3 times**

This should total 2 1/2 hours of freezing.
- **You can choose to either beat your ice cream mixture every 40 minutes until frozen or let your ice cream mixture freeze on its own.**

Either method works fine. The more you beat it, the softer it will be.
Total freezing time can take anywhere between 3-5 hours.
- **Add mix-ins to your ice cream.**

If you want to add mix-ins to your homemade ice cream, wait until the ice cream is thick enough to "hold" the mix-ins so they don't fall to the bottom of the container.

Generally, add mix-ins after 2-3 hours of freezing.

ICE CREAM MAKING TIPS

Using your ice cream maker properly will help you make delicious homemade ice cream that rivals and surpasses store-bought ice cream!

Here are some helpful tips to get you started. First, let me state the most important rule...

Always, always, always follow the manufacturer's instructions!

Obvious, I know, but I had to mention it! This will lengthen the life of your machine, ensure that you clean it properly, and ultimately help you produce better ice cream.

Now that we've got that covered - let's move on to some more ice cream maker tips - hopefully ones that are a little less basic!

Prep Tips

Make sure that the ice cream base is already cold before putting it into the ice cream machine.
Why? Ice cream is smoother and tastes better when it freezes faster.

Consider mixing your ice cream base the night before and let the base sit in the fridge overnight.
Why? Letting the flavors blend together can enhance the flavor of the ice cream.

Making Tips
When adding ice cream to your maker, only fill the ice cream maker bowl about 2/3 full.
Why? Air is added to the ice cream as it churns, so there needs to be room for the ice cream to expand!

Consider pre-freezing mix-ins before adding them to your ice cream.
Why? This will prevent them from warming up the ice cream - remember a faster, more consistent freeze produces better ice cream!

Generally, add mix-ins during the last 5 minutes of churning.
Why? If you add them too soon they will tend to sink to the bottom.

Make sure that mix-ins are chopped well and chunks are not too big.
Why? Large chunks can damage your machine. A good rule of thumb is that mix-ins should not be bigger in size than a chocolate chip. Soft mix-ins, like thinly sliced fruit can be a little larger.

If your ice cream machine's bowl is made out of metal, do not scoop out the ice cream with a metal utensil.
Why? This will scratch the container. I like to use a plastic spoon, but a plastic or wood utensil will work fine.

Storing Tips

Transfer completed ice cream from your ice cream machine to a pre-chilled container.
Why? This prevents the ice cream from melting during the transfer.

Place ice cream in a metal bowl or a bowl covered with foil.
Why? This freezes ice cream faster and keeps ice cream frozen better. Don't forget a fast, consistent freeze produces the best ice cream.

Don't let your ice cream melt and then refreeze it.
Why? Not only is this a potential health hazard, it also makes the ice cream hard and full of ice crystals!

Always store ice cream covered and never store ice cream next to uncovered food.
Why? It can absorb the flavor of other foods!

Store ice cream between -5 to 0 degrees C.
Why? This is a happy balance between proper storage and easy scooping.

I hope these tips help you make the best homemade ice cream your ice cream maker can possibly churn out!

CLASSIC RECIPES

CARMEL ICE CREAM RECIPE

Philadelphia Style

Prep Time: 25 minutes
Chill Time: 2 hours
Ice Cream Maker Time: Approximately 25-30 minutes
Makes: 1 ½ quarts
Servings: Ten ½ cup servings

Ingredients:
1 cup granulated sugar
1 cup milk
2 cups heavy whipping cream

Directions:

1. Place sugar in a large heavy saucepan (the saucepan must be large).
2. Cook sugar over medium heat, stirring constantly until sugar melts into a liquid and turns a golden brown color.
3. Remove from heat.
4. Slowly and carefully, add milk to caramelized sugar.
5. **Be careful – the mixture will splatter and the sugar will turn hard. Don't worry!**
6. Stir mixture over low heat until it becomes smooth again.
7. Mix in whipping cream and stir until well mixed and smooth.
8. Remove from heat and allow mixture to cool.
9. Once cool, chill mixture in the fridge for at least 2 hours.
10. Pour chilled mixture into your ice cream maker.
11. Mix about 25-30 minutes or according to manufacturer's instructions.

CARMEL ICE CREAM RECIPE

Custard Style

Prep Time: 30 minutes
Chill Time: 2 hours
Ice Cream Maker Time: Approximately 25-30 minutes
Makes: 1 ½ quarts
Servings: Ten ½ cup servings

Ingredients:

2 eggs
1 cup granulated sugar
1 cup milk
2 cups heavy whipping cream

Directions:

1. Beat eggs until they are light and fluffy. Set eggs aside.
2. In a large heavy saucepan (the saucepan must be large!), heat sugar over medium heat. Be sure to stir constantly.
3. Sugar will melt and turn into a golden brown liquid.
4. When this happens, remove from heat.
5. Carefully and slowly, pour milk into saucepan with caramelized sugar.
6. **Be careful – the mixture will splatter and the sugar will turn hard. Don't worry!**
7. Over low heat, stir mixture until sugar melts again and the mixture becomes smooth.
8. Add whipping cream and stir until mixture is smooth and blended.
9. Pour some of the warm mixture over the beaten eggs and mix well.
10. Pour egg mixture back into saucepan and continue to cook over low heat until mixture thickens and begins to stick to the back of your spoon.
11. Remove saucepan from heat and allow mixture to cool.
12. Once cool, chill mixture in the fridge for at least 2 hours.
13. Once mixture is totally chilled, pour into your ice cream maker.
14. Churn about 25-30 minutes or according to manufacturer's instructions.

COFFEE ICE CREAM RECIPE

Philadelphia Style

Prep Time: 10 minutes
Ice Cream Maker Time: Approximately 25-30 minutes
Makes: 1 ½ quarts
Servings: Ten ½ cup servings

Ingredients:
1 cup milk
½ cup granulated sugar
3 tbsp instant coffee (2 – 2 ½ tbsp instant coffee for a "weaker" ice cream)
2 cups heavy cream
1 tsp vanilla extract

Directions:

1. Mix milk, sugar, and coffee with an electric mixer or whisk so that sugar and coffee dissolve in the milk.
2. Add cream and vanilla and stir.
3. Pour into your ice cream maker.
4. Mix until thick about 25-30 minutes or according to manufacturer's instructions.

COFFEE ICE CREAM RECIPE

Custard Style

Prep Time: 10 minutes
Chill Time: 2 hours
Ice Cream Maker Time: Approximately 25-30 minutes
Makes: 1 ½ quarts
Servings: Ten ½ cup servings

Ingredients:
1 cup milk
2 cups heavy cream
2/3 cup granulated sugar
3 tbsp instant coffee (2 – 2 ½ tbsp instant coffee for a "weaker" ice cream)
4 egg yolks

Directions:

1. Mix milk, cream, sugar, and coffee in a saucepan over medium heat, heating until mixture just begins to boil.
2. In a separate bowl, beat egg yolks.
3. Pour hot cream mixture over beaten eggs, mixing well.
4. Return mixture to saucepan, cooking on medium-low heat until mixture thickens and begins to stick to the back of your spoon.
5. Remove from heat and chill in refrigerator for at least 2 hours.
6. Pour chilled mixture into your ice cream maker.
7. Mix until thick about 25-30 minutes or according to manufacturer's instructions.

GREEN TEA ICE CREAM RECIPE

Philadelphia Style

Prep Time: 15 minutes
Chill Time: 3 hours
Ice Cream Maker Time: Approximately 20-25 minutes
Makes: 1 ½ quarts
Servings: Ten ½ cup servings

Ingredients:

1 ¼ cup milk
2 tbsp loose leaf green tea (equivalent to 3 green tea bags)
½ cup granulated sugar
2 cups heavy whipping cream
1 tsp vanilla extract
4 tsp lemon juice

Directions:

1. Stirring frequently, heat milk until it just begins to bubble.
2. Remove from heat.
3. Steep green tea in hot milk for 5 minutes.
4. Strain green tea from milk or remove tea bags.
5. Dissolve sugar in hot milk.
6. Cool in refrigerator for 3 hours.
7. Stir in cream, vanilla, and lemon juice.
8. Pour mixture into your ice cream maker.
9. Churn about 20-25 minutes or according to manufacturer's instructions.

***Helpful Hint:** To vary the intensity of the green tea flavor, you can change the length of time that you steep the tea.
Steeping the green tea for 5 minutes produces my favorite flavor. Steeping the green tea for only 3 minutes produces a weak green tea flavor. Steeping the green tea for 7 minutes produces a strong green tea flavor.

GREEN TEA ICE CREAM RECIPE

Custard Style

Prep Time: 15 minutes
Chill Time: 3 hours
Ice Cream Maker Time: Approximately 20-25 minutes
Makes: 1 ½ quarts
Servings: Ten ½ cup servings

Ingredients:

3 eggs
2/3 cup sugar
2 tbsp matcha green tea powder
2 cups whipping cream
1 cup milk
¼ tsp salt

Directions:

1. In a medium bowl, whisk eggs, sugar, and matcha together.
2. In a medium saucepan, bring whipping cream, milk, and salt just to a boil.
3. Remove from heat.
4. Pour 1 cup of the hot cream mixture over the whisked eggs and beat well.
5. Pour the egg mixture back into the saucepan and continue to cook over medium low heat.
6. Continue to stir until mixture becomes thick and begins to stick to the back of your spoon.
7. Pour the ice cream base through a sieve and cool.
8. Once it has cooled to room temperature, cover and chill the ice cream in the fridge for about 3 hours or until cold.
9. Pour chilled mixture into your ice cream machine and churn about 20-25 minutes or according to manufacturer's instructions.

PEANUT BUTTER ICE CREAM RECIPE

Philadelphia Style

Prep Time: 10 minutes
Ice Cream Maker Time: Approximately 25-30 minutes
Makes: 1 ½ quarts
Servings: Ten ½ cup servings

Ingredients:

1 cup creamy peanut butter
½ cup granulated sugar
1 cup milk
2 cups heavy cream
1 tsp vanilla extract

Directions:

1. Cream peanut butter and sugar together until mixed.
2. Stir peanut butter mixture and milk together until smooth and sugar is completely dissolved (use a whisk or hand mixer).
3. Add cream and vanilla and stir well.
4. Pour mixture into your ice cream maker.
5. Mix until thick about 25-30 minutes or according to manufacturer's instructions.

PEANUT BUTTER ICE CREAM RECIPE

Custard Style

Prep Time: 10 minutes
Chill Time: at least 2 hours
Ice Cream Maker Time: Approximately 25-30 minutes
Makes: 1 ½ quarts
Servings: Ten ½ cup servings

Ingredients:

1 cup milk
3 eggs
¾ cup granulated sugar
2 cups heavy whipping cream
¾ cup creamy peanut butter
2 tsp vanilla extract

Directions:

1. Beat eggs until they are light and fluffy.
2. Gradually, whisk sugar into eggs. Set aside.
3. In a saucepan, heat milk until it just begins to boil.
4. Pour hot milk over beaten eggs. Stir well.
5. Return mixture to saucepan and heat over low heat, but do not allow it to boil.
6. Stir constantly until the mixture begins to stick to the back of your spoon and becomes thick. Remove from heat.
7. Stir in peanut butter until completely blended.
8. Cool and chill in refrigerator for at least 2 hours until cold.
9. Add cream and vanilla to cooled mixture.
10. Pour into ice cream maker.
11. Mix until thick about 25-30 minutes or according to manufacturer's instructions.

PEPPERMINT ICE CREAM RECIPE

Philadelphia Style

Prep Time: 10 minutes
Ice Cream Maker Time: Approximately 25-30 minutes
Makes: 1 ½ quarts
Servings: Ten ½ cup servings

Ingredients:
1 cup milk
2/3 cup granulated sugar
2 cups whipping cream
½ tsp vanilla extract
½ tsp peppermint extract
2/3 cup crushed hard peppermint candies
½ cup dark chocolate sticks (optional)

Directions:
1. With a whisk, mix milk and sugar together so that the sugar dissolves completely.
2. Add heavy whipping cream, vanilla, and peppermint extract and stir until completely blended.
3. Pour this mixture into your ice cream maker.
4. Churn in ice cream maker about 20-25 minutes or according to manufacturer's instructions.
5. Add crushed hard peppermint candy to churning mixture.
6. Churn for an additional 5 minutes.
7. Transfer peppermint ice cream to storage container and mix in chocolate sticks, if desired.

Helpful Hint: What texture do you want? You can either grind up the peppermint candies to a powder or coarsely crush candies into small peppermint chunks. Be careful not to make the chunks too big or they may damage your ice cream maker.

PEPPERMINT ICE CREAM RECIPE

Custard Style

Prep Time: 25 minutes
Chill Time: 2 hours
Ice Cream Maker Time: Approximately 25-30 minutes
Makes: 1 ½ quarts
Servings: Ten ½ cup servings

Ingredients:
2 eggs
2/3 cup granulated sugar
1 cup milk
2 cups whipping cream
½ tsp vanilla extract
½ tsp peppermint extract
2/3 cup crushed hard peppermint candies
½ cup dark chocolate sticks (optional)

Directions:
1. Place eggs in a small bowl and beat well with sugar.
2. In a saucepan, heat milk until it starts to bubble.
3. Pour hot milk over beaten egg mixture. Stir well.
4. Pour this mixture back into saucepan and heat, stirring constantly until mixture becomes thick and sticks to the back of a spoon.
5. Chill for at least 2 hours.
6. After mixture is chilled, stir in cream, vanilla, and peppermint extract.
7. Pour this ice cream base into your ice cream machine.
8. Mix for 20-25 minutes (or according to manufacturer's instructions).
9. Into the churning ice cream, pour the crushed peppermint candies.
10. Mix 5 more minutes.
11. As you transfer the ice cream to another container, stir in chocolate sticks, if desired.

Helpful Hint: Depending on what texture you like, you can grind the peppermint candies up almost into powder or you can coarsely crush them for small peppermint chunks in your ice cream. Just be sure that the chunks aren't too big or they may hurt your ice cream maker.

VANILLA ICE CREAM RECIPE

Philadelphia Style

Prep Time: 7 minutes
Ice Cream Maker Time: Approximately 20-25 minutes
Makes: 1 ½ quarts
Servings: Ten ½ cup servings

Ingredients:
1 cup milk
½ cup granulated sugar
2 cups heavy whipping cream
1 ½ - 2 tsp vanilla extract

Directions:

1. Mix milk and sugar with a wire whisk or hand mixer (low speed for 1-2 minutes) in a medium bowl until sugar dissolves.
2. Gently stir in heavy cream and vanilla.
3. Pour mixture into your ice cream maker.
4. Mix about 20-25 minutes or according to manufacturer's instructions.

VANILLA ICE CREAM RECIPE

Custard Style

Prep Time: 10 minutes
Chill Time: at least 3 hours
Ice Cream Maker Time: Approximately 20-25 minutes
Makes: 1 ½ quarts
Servings: Ten ½ cup servings

Ingredients:
2 large eggs
½ cup granulated sugar
1 cup milk
2 cups heavy cream
1 ½ - 2 tsp vanilla extract

Directions:

1. Whisk eggs for 1-2 minutes until they are light and fluffy.
2. Gradually, whisk in sugar, then whisk for 1 minute more.
3. In a saucepan, heat milk until it just starts to bubble.
4. Pour hot milk mixture over eggs and beat well.
5. Pour milk back into saucepan and continue to heat over low heat, stirring constantly.
6. Continue to heat until mixture starts to thicken and begins to stick to the back of your spoon.
7. Remove from heat, cool and then chill in fridge for at least 3 hours until completely cooled.
8. Add cream and vanilla, stirring until completely blended.
9. Pour this mixture into your ice cream maker.
10. Mix about 20-25 minutes or according to manufacturer's directions.

Choco-holic Recipes

CHOCOLATE ICE CREAM RECIPE

Philadelphia Style

Prep Time: 10 minutes
Chill Time: about 2 hours
Ice Cream Maker Time: Approximately 25-30 minutes
Makes: 1 ½ quarts
Servings: Ten ½ cup servings

Ingredients:
1 cup milk
½ cup granulated sugar
1 1/3 cup bittersweet/semi-sweet chocolate
2 cups heavy cream
1 tsp vanilla extract

Directions:

1. Heat milk (stove or microwave) until it just begins to bubble.
2. Meanwhile, process chocolate in a food processor or blender until the chocolate is finely chopped.
3. Mix chocolate and sugar.
4. Combine hot milk and chocolate mixture and blend until chocolate is melted and the mixture is smooth.
5. Cool.
6. Once cool, stir in heavy cream and vanilla.
7. Chill for at least 2 hours.
8. Pour mixture into your ice cream maker.
9. Mix in ice cream machine for 25-30 minutes or according to manufacturer's instructions.

CHOCOLATE ICE CREAM RECIPE

Custard Style

Prep Time: 15 minutes
Chill Time: 3 hours
Ice Cream Maker Time: Approximately 25-30 minutes
Makes: 1 quart
Servings: Eight ½ cup servings

Ingredients:

2 oz (1/3 cup) unsweetened chocolate
1/3 cup unsweetened cocoa powder
1 ½ cups milk
2 large eggs
1 cup sugar
1 cup heavy cream
1 tsp vanilla extract

Directions:

1. Whisk eggs for 1-2 minutes or until light and fluffy.
2. Gradually stir in sugar and whisk. Set aside.
3. In a double boiler, melt unsweetened chocolate.
4. Add cocoa powder, stirring constantly until smooth.
5. Using a whisk, stir in milk until smooth and blended.
6. Heat until mixture starts to bubble.
7. Pour mixture over eggs and mix together.
8. Pour mixture back into saucepan and heat on low, stirring constantly until mixture thickens and begins to stick to the back of your spoon.
9. Remove from heat, cool, and chill in fridge for at least 3 hours, until completely cooled.
10. Blend in heavy cream and vanilla.
11. Pour into your ice cream maker.
12. Mix in ice cream machine for 25-30 minutes or according to manufacturer's instructions.

CHOCOLATE CHIP COOKIE DOUGH ICE CREAM RECIPE

Philadelphia Style

Prep Time: 20 minutes
Ice Cream Maker Time: Approximately 20-25 minutes
Makes: 1 ½ quarts
Servings: Ten ½ cup servings

Ingredients:

1 cup milk
½ cup granulated sugar
2 cups heavy whipping cream
1 ½ tsp vanilla extract
½ cup chocolate chips
½ cup cookie dough shaped into small balls*
*To make Cookie Dough see bottom of page

Directions:

1. Mix milk and sugar until the sugar dissolves (about 1-2 minutes – a hand mixer or whisk works well).
2. Add heavy cream and vanilla extract.
3. Pour mixture into the ice cream maker.
4. Mix in ice cream maker about 15-20 minutes or according to manufacturer's instructions.
5. Meanwhile, prepare cookie dough.*
6. Add chocolate chips and cookie dough balls to ice cream mixture.
7. Mix for 5 more minutes in ice cream maker.

*Cookie Dough Instructions

½ cup butter
½ cup brown sugar
¼ cup granulated sugar
½ tsp vanilla
1 cup flour
½ tsp salt
Cream butter, sugars, and vanilla until blended.
Add flour and salt. Stir until well mixed.
Form into small balls.

CHOCOLATE CHIP COOKIE DOUGH
ICE CREAM RECIPE

Custard Style

Prep Time: 20 minutes
Chill Time: 3 hours
Ice Cream Maker Time: Approximately 20-25 minutes
Makes: 1 ½ quarts
Servings: Ten ½ cup servings

Ingredients:

2 large eggs
¼ cup sugar
1 cup milk
2 cups whipping cream
*To make Cookie Dough see bottom of page

1 ½ - 2 tsp vanilla extract
½ cup chocolate chips
½ cup cookie dough shaped into
small balls*

Directions:

1. Beat eggs for 1-2 minutes so they become light and fluffy.
2. Stir in sugar and whisk.
3. In a saucepan, heat milk until it just begins to bubble.
4. Pour heated milk over beaten eggs and mix well.
5. Pour the milk/egg mixture back into the saucepan.
6. Continue to heat over low heat, stirring constantly until mixture thickens and begins to stick to the back of your spoon.
7. Remove from heat and chill in fridge for about 3 hours until mixture cools completely.
8. Stir in cream, and vanilla until completely blended.
9. Pour into your ice cream maker and churn in ice cream maker about 15-20 minutes or according to manufacturer's instructions.
10. Meanwhile, prepare cookie dough.*
11. Add chocolate chips and cookie dough balls to ice cream mixture.
12. Mix for 5 more minutes in ice cream maker.

*Cookie Dough Instructions

½ cup butter
½ cup brown sugar
¼ cup granulated sugar

½ tsp vanilla
1 cup flour
½ tsp salt

Cream butter, sugars, and vanilla until blended.
Add flour and salt. Stir until well mixed.
Form into small balls.

CHOCOLATE COOKIE ICE CREAM RECIPE

Philadelphia Style

Prep Time: 15 minutes
Chill Time: 3 hours
Ice Cream Maker Time: Approximately 25-30 minutes
Makes: 1 ½ quarts
Servings: Ten ½ cup servings

Ingredients:
1 cup milk
½ cup granulated sugar
1 1/3 cup bittersweet or semi-sweet chocolate (8 oz)
2 cups heavy cream
1 tsp vanilla extract
¾ cup crushed cookies*
*Crushed Cookies: You can use Oreos, graham crackers, chocolate chip cookies, or vanilla wafers. Place cookies in a Ziploc bag. Seal. Crush cookies with the heel of your hand.

Directions:

1. Using your stovetop or microwave, heat milk until it begins to bubble around the edges.
2. In the mean time, chop the chocolate in a blender or food processor until it is chopped into fine pieces.
3. Combine chocolate and sugar.
4. Stir chocolate mixture and hot milk together until smooth.
5. Let this mixture cool.
6. Stir in heavy cream and vanilla to cooled mixture.
7. Chill in fridge for 3 hours until completely cool.
8. Pour mixture into ice cream machine.
9. Churn about 20-25 minutes or according to manufacturer's instructions.
10. Add crushed cookies to chocolate ice cream.
11. Churn an additional 5 minutes.

CHOCOLATE COOKIE ICE CREAM RECIPE

Custard Style

Prep Time: 15 minutes
Chill Time: 3 hours
Ice Cream Maker Time: Approximately 25-30 minutes
Makes: 1 quart
Servings: Eight ½ cup servings

Ingredients:
2 oz (1/3 cup) unsweetened chocolate
1/3 cup unsweetened cocoa powder
1 ½ cups milk
2 large eggs
1 cup granulated sugar
1 cup heavy cream
1 tsp vanilla extract
¾ cup crushed cookies*

*Crushed Cookies: Oreos, chocolate chip cookies, graham crackers, or vanilla wafers work well. Place the cookies of your choice in a Ziploc bag. Close securely. Crush with the heel of your hand or with a rolling pin.

Directions:

1. Whisk eggs until they are light and fluffy (1-2 minutes).
2. Gradually stir in sugar and whisk for 1 minute.
3. Melt unsweetened chocolate, using a double boiler.
4. Add cocoa powder and stir constantly until mixture is smooth.
5. Add milk, stirring with a whisk until mixture is smooth and blended.
6. Heat until mixture begins to bubble then pour over whisked eggs.
7. Stir together and then return to saucepan.
8. Heat on low, stirring constantly until mixture thickens and sticks to the back of your spoon.
9. Remove from heat and chill until cool – about 3 hours.
10. Add heavy cream and vanilla.
11. Pour into your ice cream maker.
12. Mix in ice cream machine for 20-25 minutes or according to manufacturer's instructions.
13. Add crushed cookies to chocolate ice cream.
14. Churn an additional 5 minutes.

CHOCOLATE GOAT MILK
ICE CREAM RECIPE

Philadelphia Style

Prep Time: 15 minutes
Ice Cream Maker Time: Approximately 20-25 minutes
Makes: 1 ½ quarts
Servings: Ten ½ cup servings

Ingredients:

¼ cup powdered unsweetened cocoa
½ cup sugar
¼ teaspoon salt
1 cup goat milk
2 cups heavy cream
1 teaspoon vanilla
½ cup chocolate chips (optional)

Directions:

1. Mix the cocoa, sugar, and salt together in a medium mixing bowl.
2. Whisk in the goat milk and stir until sugar is completely dissolved and cocoa is blended.
3. Stir in heavy cream and vanilla.
4. Pour into ice cream maker.
5. Churn about 15-20 minutes or according to manufacturer's instructions.
6. Add chocolate chips, if desired.
7. Churn an additional 5 minutes.

CHOCOLATE GOAT MILK
ICE CREAM RECIPE

Custard Style

Prep Time: 15 minutes
Chill Time: at least 3 hours
Ice Cream Maker Time: Approximately 25-30 minutes
Makes: 1 ½ quarts
Servings: Ten ½ cup servings

Ingredients:
¼ cup powdered unsweetened cocoa
½ cup sugar
¼ teaspoon salt
1 cup goat milk
2 egg yolks, lightly beaten
2 cups whipping cream
1 teaspoon vanilla
½ cup chocolate chips (optional)

Directions:

1. Stir cocoa, sugar, and salt together in a saucepan, and add goat milk and whisk.
2. Over medium heat, warm this mixture until it begins to bubble.
3. Beat egg yolks.
4. Pour the goat's milk mixture over the egg yolks and whisk.
5. Pour back into the saucepan.
6. Stirring constantly, heat this egg mixture over low-medium heat until it thickens and begins to stick to the back of your spoon.
7. Place in fridge until chilled (about 3 hours).
8. Stir in the whipping cream and vanilla.
9. Churn in your ice cream machine about 15-20 minutes or according to manufacturer's instructions.
10. Add chocolate chips if desired.
11. Churn an additional 5 minutes.

COOKIES & CREAM ICE CREAM RECIPE

Philadelphia Style

Prep Time: 8 minutes
Ice Cream Maker Time: Approximately 20-25 minutes
Makes: 1 ½ quarts
Servings: Ten ½ cup servings

Ingredients:
1 cup milk
½ cup granulated sugar
2 cups heavy whipping cream
1 ½ tsp vanilla extract
¾ cup crushed Oreo cookies*
*Place Oreo cookies in a Ziploc bag. Seal bag. Crush cookies using the heel of your hand.

Directions:

1. Using a wire whisk or hand mixer, mix milk and sugar until the sugar dissolves (about 1-2 minutes).
2. Stir in heavy cream and vanilla extract.
3. Pour into ice cream maker.
4. Churn about 15-20 minutes or according to manufacturer's instructions.
5. Add crushed Oreo cookies to ice cream.
6. Churn for 5 additional minutes.

COOKIES & CREAM ICE CREAM RECIPE

Custard Style

Prep Time: 8 minutes
Ice Cream Maker Time: Approximately 20-25 minutes
Makes: 1 ½ quarts
Servings: Ten ½ cup servings

Ingredients:
2 large eggs
¼ cup sugar
1 cup milk
2 cups heavy whipping cream
1 ½ - 2 tsp vanilla extract
¾ cup crushed Oreo cookies*
*Place Oreo cookies in a Ziploc bag. Seal bag. Crush cookies using the heel of your hand.

Directions:

1. Whisk eggs until they are light and fluffy.
2. Stir in sugar gradually and then whisk for 1 additional minute.
3. Add milk, cream, and vanilla and stir until completely mixed.
4. Pour this mixture into your ice cream maker.
5. Mix about 15-20 minutes or according to manufacturer's instructions.
6. Add crushed Oreo cookies.
7. Churn for 5 additional minutes.

DIRT ICE CREAM RECIPE

Philadelphia Style

Prep Time: 15 minutes
Chill Time: 3 hours
Ice Cream Maker Time: Approximately 25-30 minutes
Makes: 1 ½ quarts
Servings: Ten ½ cup servings

Ingredients:
1 cup milk
1/3 cup granulated sugar
1 1/3 cup bittersweet or semi-sweet chocolate (8 oz)
2 cups heavy cream
1 tsp vanilla extract
½ cup crushed Oreos (about 5 cookies)
½ cup gummy worms
*Crushed Oreos: Put Oreos in a Ziploc bag. Carefully close the bag. With the heel of your hand, crush Oreos.

Directions:

1. Heat milk until it just begins to bubble (in microwave or on stove).
2. Chop chocolate into fine pieces using a food processor or blender.
3. Combine chocolate and sugar.
4. Blend hot milk and chocolate mixture until mixture is smooth and chocolate is melted.
5. Let the chocolate mixture cool.
6. Stir in cream and vanilla.
7. Let this mixture chill for 3 hours or until cooled.
8. Pour into your ice cream maker.
9. Mix about 20-25 minutes or according to manufacturer's instructions.
10. Add crushed Oreo.
11. Mix about 5 more minutes in your ice cream maker.
12. Place ice cream in an airtight container for storage.
13. Stir in gummy worms with a large spoon.

Helpful Hint: Do not put gummy worms into ice cream maker. Because of their size, they may harm your machine.

DIRT ICE CREAM RECIPE

Custard Style

Prep Time: 15 minutes
Chill Time: 3 hours
Ice Cream Maker Time: Approximately 25-30 minutes
Makes: 1 quart
Servings: Eight ½ cup servings

Ingredients:
2 oz (1/3 cup) unsweetened chocolate
1/3 cup unsweetened cocoa powder
1 ½ cups milk
2 large eggs
1 cup granulated sugar
1 cup heavy cream
1 tsp vanilla extract
½ cup crushed Oreos (about 5 cookies)
½ cup gummy worms
*Crushed Oreos: Put Oreos in a Ziploc bag. Carefully close the bag. With the heel of your hand, crush Oreos.

Directions:

1. Whisk eggs until light and fluffy, slowly stir in sugar and whisk again.
2. Using a double boiler, melt chocolate.
3. Slowly pour in cocoa powder, stirring until completely smooth.
4. With a whisk, stir in milk so mixture is blended and smooth.
5. Heat until mixture just begins to bubble and then pour over eggs.
6. Beat and then return to saucepan.
7. Heat over low heat until mixture thickens and begins to stick to the back of your spoon.
8. Remove from heat. Allow to cool and then chill for at least 3 hours.
9. Mix in cream and vanilla.
10. Pour into ice cream maker and churn for 20-25 minutes or according to manufacturer's instructions.
11. Add crushed Oreo.
12. Churn an additional 5 minutes in your ice cream maker.
13. Place ice cream in an airtight container for storage, stirring in gummy worms with a large spoon.

Helpful Hint: Because of their size, gummy worms may harm your machine. Don't put gummy worms into ice cream maker – hand stir them into your ice cream.

MINT CHOCOLATE CHIP
ICE CREAM RECIPE

Philadelphia Style

Prep Time: 7 minutes
Ice Cream Maker Time: Approximately 20-25 minutes
Makes: 1 ½ quarts
Servings: Ten ½ cup servings

Ingredients:
1 cup milk
½ cup granulated sugar
2 cups heavy whipping cream
1 - 1 ½ tsp peppermint extract
¾ cup chocolate chips *or* 4 oz chopped semi-sweet chocolate

Directions:

1. Dissolve milk and sugar using a wire whisk or hand mixer (mix approximately 1 -2 minutes).
2. Stir in heavy cream and peppermint extract.
3. Pour mixture into your ice cream maker.
4. Mix about 15-20 minutes.
5. Add chocolate to the ice cream mixture.
6. Mix 5 minutes.

MINT CHOCOLATE CHIP
ICE CREAM RECIPE

Custard Style

Prep Time: 25 minutes
Chill Time: 3 hours
Ice Cream Maker Time: Approximately 25-30 minutes
Makes: 1 ½ quarts
Servings: Ten ½ cup servings

Ingredients:

2 eggs
1 cup milk
½ cup granulated sugar
2 cups whipping cream
1 ½ tsp peppermint extract
¾ cup chocolate chips **or** 4 oz chopped semi-sweet chocolate

Directions:

1. Place eggs and sugar in a small bowl and beat until light and fluffy. Set aside.
2. In a saucepan, heat milk until it just starts to bubble.
3. Pour hot milk over beaten egg mixture. Stir well.
4. Pour this mixture back into saucepan and heat, stirring constantly until mixture becomes thick and sticks to the back of a spoon.
5. Chill for at least 3 hours.
6. After mixture is chilled, stir in heavy whipping cream and peppermint extract.
7. Pour into your ice cream machine.
8. Mix for 20-25 minutes (or according to manufacturer's instructions).
9. Add chocolate chips to the churning ice cream.
10. Churn an additional 5 minutes.

ROCKY ROAD ICE CREAM RECIPE

Philadelphia Style

Prep Time: 15 minutes
Chill Time: 3 hours
Ice Cream Maker Time: Approximately 25-30 minutes
Makes: 1 ½ quarts
Servings: Ten ½ cup servings

Ingredients:
1 cup milk
½ cup granulated sugar
1 1/3 cup bittersweet or semi-sweet chocolate (8 oz)
2 cups heavy cream
1 tsp vanilla extract
½ cup chopped pecans or almonds
¼ cup chocolate chunks or chocolate chips
¾ cup mini marshmallows

Directions:

1. On your stove or in your microwave, heat milk until it just starts to bubble.
2. While the milk is heating, finely chop chocolate in a food processor or blender.
3. Stir chopped chocolate and sugar together.
4. Blend hot milk and chocolate together until chocolate completely melts and the mixture is smooth.
5. Cool in refrigerator for at least 15 minutes.
6. Once cool, stir in heavy cream and vanilla.
7. Chill in fridge for at least 3 hours.
8. Pour mixture into your ice cream maker.
9. Mix about 20-25 minutes or according to manufacturer's instructions.
10. Add chopped nuts and chocolate chunks.
11. Mix in ice cream maker an additional 5 minutes.
12. Remove from ice cream maker and place in a storage container.
13. Stir in marshmallows immediately.

Helpful Hint: For best results, freeze marshmallows before stirring into ice cream.

ROCKY ROAD ICE CREAM RECIPE

Custard Style

Prep Time: 15 minutes
Chill Time: 1-2 hours
Ice Cream Maker Time: Approximately 25-30 minutes
Makes: 1 quart
Servings: Eight ½ cup servings

Ingredients:

2 oz (1/3 cup) unsweetened chocolate
1/3 cup unsweetened cocoa powder
1 ½ cups milk
2 large eggs
1 cup granulated sugar
1 cup heavy cream
1 tsp vanilla extract
1/3 cup chopped pecans or almonds
¼ cup chocolate chunks or chocolate chips
2/3 cup mini marshmallows

Directions:

1. Beat eggs 1-2 minutes until they are light and fluffy.
2. Gradually stir in sugar and whisk for 1 minute and set aside.
3. Melt chocolate in a double boiler. Slowly add cocoa powder, stirring until smooth.
4. Using a whisk, stir in milk. Stir until mixture is blended and smooth.
5. Heat until milk just begins to bubble.
6. Pour milk over eggs and beat well.
7. Return to saucepan and heat over low heat, stirring constantly until mixture sticks to back of spoon and thickens.
8. Remove from heat and chill in fridge about 3 hours.
9. Add heavy cream and vanilla extract.
10. Pour this mixture into your ice cream maker.
11. Churn for 20-25 minutes or according to manufacturer's instructions.
12. Add chopped nuts and chocolate chunks and churn 5 more minutes.
13. Remove from ice cream maker and place in a storage container.
14. Stir in marshmallows immediately.

Helpful Hint: Freeze marshmallows ahead of time so that when you stir them into your ice cream – the ice cream doesn't partially melt!

FRUIT RECIPES

BANANA ICE CREAM RECIPE

Philadelphia Style

Prep Time: 15 minutes
Ice Cream Maker Time: Approximately 25-30 minutes
Makes: 1 ½ quarts
Servings: Ten ½ cup servings

Ingredients:
¾ cup milk
½ cup sugar
¼ tsp nutmeg
3 – 4 ripe medium bananas
2 cups heavy whipping cream
1 tsp vanilla extract

Directions:

1. Mix milk, sugar, and nutmeg until sugar dissolves (a wire whisk or hand mixer works well).
2. Mash or puree bananas until the bananas are pureed.
3. Stir bananas into milk mixture.
4. For best freezing results, chill banana/milk mixture for at least 1 hour.
5. Add whipping cream and vanilla.
6. Stir well.
7. Pour mixture into ice cream maker.
8. Churn about 25-30 minutes or according to manufacturer's instructions.

BANANA ICE CREAM RECIPE

Custard Style

Prep Time: 15 minutes
Chill Time: at least 3 hours
Ice Cream Maker Time: Approximately 25-30 minutes
Makes: 1 ½ quarts
Servings: Ten ½ cup servings

Ingredients:
1 cup milk
1 cup sugar
2 eggs, beaten
2 ripe bananas
2 cups heavy whipping cream
½ tsp vanilla
¼ tsp nutmeg

Directions:

1. Mix milk, sugar, and beaten eggs in a saucepan.
2. Over low heat, stir milk mixture until it begins to thicken.
3. Chill in fridge until cool – at least 3 hours.
4. Meanwhile, mash or puree bananas.
5. When custard base is cool, stir in pureed bananas, whipping cream, vanilla, and nutmeg.
6. Pour into your ice cream maker.
7. Churn about 25-30 minutes or according to manufacturer's instructions.
8. Add toppings if desired and enjoy!

BLACKBERRY ICE CREAM RECIPE

Philadelphia Style

Prep Time: 15 minutes
Fridge: 2 - 24 hours
Ice Cream Maker Time: Approximately 25-30 minutes
Makes: 1 ½ quarts
Servings: Ten ½ cup servings

Ingredients:

Blackberries
1 pint (2 cups) blackberries (fresh or frozen)
¾ cup sugar

Ice Cream Base
¾ cup sugar
¾ cup milk
2 cups heavy whipping cream

Directions:

Blackberries
1. In a food processor or blender, process berries with sugar until smooth.
2. Place blackberry mixture in the fridge for at least 2 hours. Leaving the blackberries, in the fridge longer will enhance the flavor, so I kept mine in the fridge overnight.
3. If desired, strain seeds from blackberries.

Ice Cream
1. Mix milk and sugar together so that sugar dissolves.
2. Add whipping cream and combine well.
3. Stir in blackberry mixture.
4. Pour into your ice cream machine.
5. Churn about 25-30 minutes or according to manufacturer's instructions.

BLACKBERRY ICE CREAM RECIPE

Custard Style

Prep Time: 15 minutes
Chill Time: at least 3 hours
Ice Cream Maker Time: Approximately 25-30 minutes
Makes: 1 ½ quarts
Servings: Ten ½ cup servings

Ingredients:

Blackberries
1 pint (2 cups) blackberries (fresh or frozen)
¾ cup sugar

Ice Cream 2 eggs
¾ cup sugar
¾ cup milk
2 cups heavy whipping cream

Directions:

Blackberries
1. In a blender or food processor, process berries with sugar until smooth.
2. Place blackberry mixture in the fridge for at least 2 hours for flavors to blend. Leaving the blackberries, in the fridge longer enhances the flavor, so I kept mine in the fridge overnight.
3. If desired, strain seeds from blackberry mixture.

Ice Cream
1. Meanwhile, beat eggs with remaining ¾ cup sugar until the mixture is a pale yellow color.
2. Heat milk just until bubbles start to form.
3. Pour the hot milk over the beaten eggs. Lightly whisk.
4. Pour this egg/milk mixture back into the saucepan. Over medium heat, stir until mixture thickens and begins to stick to the back of your spoon.
5. Chill completely – this will take at least 3 hours.
6. Add whipping cream to chilled milk mixture and combine well. Stir in blackberry mixture.
7. Pour into ice cream maker. Churn about 25-30 minutes or according to manufacturer's instructions.

BLUEBERRY ICE CREAM RECIPE

Philadelphia Style

Prep Time: 20 minutes
Chill Time: 2 - 24 hours
Ice Cream Maker Time: Approximately 25-30 minutes
Makes: 1 ½ quarts
Servings: Ten ½ cup servings

Ingredients:

Blueberries
2 cups blueberries
¾ cup sugar
Pinch of salt

Ice Cream Base
½ cup milk
2 cups heavy cream
1 tsp vanilla extract

Directions:

Blueberries
1. Wash blueberries.
2. Pour blueberries into a medium saucepan and sprinkle with sugar and salt.
3. Heat over medium heat.
4. Mash berries and stir frequently for about 5 minutes.
5. Cool mixture slightly.

Ice Cream Base
1. Place blueberries in a blender and add milk.
2. Blend until smooth.
3. If you would like a smooth ice cream with no blueberry "chunks," pour this mixture through a sieve.
4. Chill until completely cooled – at least 2 hours.
5. Stir in heavy cream and vanilla.
6. Pour mixture into your ice cream maker.
7. Mix about 25-30 minutes.

BLUEBERRY ICE CREAM RECIPE

Custard Style

Prep Time: 20 minutes
Chill Time: 3 hours
Ice Cream Maker Time: Approximately 25-30 minutes
Makes: 1 ½ quarts
Servings: Ten ½ cup servings

Ingredients:
Blueberries
2 cups blueberries
¾ cup sugar
Pinch of salt
Ice Cream Base
2 large eggs
1/3 cup sugar
½ cup milk
2 cups heavy whipping cream
1 tsp vanilla extract

Directions:
Blueberries
1. Wash blueberries and place in a medium saucepan. Sprinkle with ¾ cup sugar and salt.
2. Heat over medium heat. Mash berries and stir frequently for 5 min.
3. Cool mixture slightly and place in blender and blend until smooth.
4. If you would like a smooth ice cream with no blueberry "chunks," pour this mixture through a sieve.
5. Chill until completely cooled. This will take at least 2 hours.

Ice Cream Base
1. Whisk eggs about 1-2 minutes until light and fluffy.
2. Slowly whisk in 1/3 sugar until completely blended and then whisk 1 more minute.
3. In a saucepan, heat milk just until it begins to bubble.
4. Pour hot milk into egg mixture and blend well.
5. Pour mixture back into saucepan and heat over low heat. Stir constantly until the mixture thickens and starts to stick to spoon.
6. Chill the custard base about 3 hours – until it too has completely cooled.
7. When both the blueberries and the milk mixture have cooled, stir in the heavy cream, and vanilla. Mix well.
8. Churn this mixture about 25-30 minutes or according to manufacturer's instructions.

CANTALOUPE ICE CREAM RECIPE

Philadelphia Style

Prep Time: 15 minutes
Chill Time: 1 hour
Ice Cream Maker Time: Approximately 25-30 minutes
Makes: 1 ½ quarts
Servings: Ten ½ cup servings

Ingredients:

Cantaloupe
1 ripe cantaloupe
¼ cup lemon juice
¼ cup sugar

Ice Cream Base
1 cup milk
2/3 cup granulated sugar
2 cups heavy cream
1 tsp vanilla extract

Directions:

Cantaloupe
1. Puree cantaloupe.
2. Combine cantaloupe, lemon juice, and ¼ cup sugar in a small, airtight container.
3. Chill cantaloupe mixture in the fridge for at least 1 hour.

Ice Cream Base
1. Mix milk and sugar together so that the sugar dissolves (about 1-2 minutes with a hand mixer or whisk).
2. Drain cantaloupe puree and add juice to milk mixture. Set cantaloupe aside.
3. Stir in cream and vanilla extract.
4. Pour into ice cream maker.
5. Mix about 20-25 minutes.
6. Drain cantaloupe puree again, discarding juice or saving for another use.
7. Add cantaloupe puree (not juice) to ice cream mixture.
8. Mix 5 more minutes in your ice cream maker.

CANTALOUPE ICE CREAM RECIPE

Custard Style

Prep Time: 15 minutes
Chill Time: 3 hours
Ice Cream Maker Time: Approximately 25-30 minutes
Makes: 1 ½ quarts
Servings: Ten ½ cup servings

Ingredients:
Cantaloupe
1 ripe cantaloupe
¼ cup lemon juice
¼ cup sugar

Ice Cream Base
2 eggs
¾ cup sugar
1 cup milk
2 cups heavy cream
1 tsp vanilla extract

Directions:
Cantaloupe
1. Puree cantaloupe well.
2. In a small container, mix together cantaloupe, lemon juice, and ¼ cup sugar. Chill cantaloupe puree for at least 1 hour in fridge.

Ice Cream Base
1. Beat eggs until they are light and fluffy (1-2 min).
2. Slowly add sugar to the eggs and beat for 1 more minute.
3. In a saucepan, heat milk until it just begins to boil.
4. Pour hot milk over beaten eggs, stirring to combine. Pour mixture back into the saucepan and heat, stirring constantly (don't let it boil).
5. Remove from heat when mixture thickens and sticks to your spoon.
6. Chill at least 3 hours.
7. Drain cantaloupe puree and add juice to milk mixture, setting cantaloupe puree aside. Stir in cream and vanilla.
8. Pour into ice cream maker. Mix about 20-25 minutes.
9. Drain cantaloupe puree again, discarding juice or saving for another use.
10. Add cantaloupe puree (not juice) to ice cream mixture.
11. Mix 5 more minutes in your ice cream maker.

CARAMEL APPLE ICE CREAM RECIPE

Philadelphia Style

Prep Time: 35 minutes
Chill Time: 3 hours
Ice Cream Maker Time: Approximately 25-30 minutes
Makes: 1 ½ quarts
Servings: Ten ½ cup servings

Ingredients:

Apples
2 medium Granny Smith Apples
2 tbsp butter
2 tbsp sugar
1 tsp cinnamon

Ice Cream Base
1 cup granulated sugar
1 cup milk
2 cups heavy whipping cream

Directions:

Apples
1. Peel, core, and chop apples into small chunks.
2. Melt butter in a large saucepan. Stir in apples and sugar and cook over medium-low to medium heat, stirring often.
3. Cook about 15 minutes or until apples are very soft.
4. Remove from heat and stir in cinnamon. Let apples cool completely.

Ice Cream Base
1. Add 1 cup granulated sugar to a large heavy saucepan. It is important for your safety that the saucepan be large!
2. Heat sugar over medium heat. Stir constantly until the sugar turns into a golden brown liquid. Remove from heat.
3. Slowly and with great care, pour milk into the liquid sugar.
4. You must be careful – the mixture will probably splatter and the sugar will probably harden. Don't worry!
5. Continue to stir over low heat until mixture becomes smooth.
6. Add whipping cream and mix until well blended.
7. Remove from heat and let cool.
8. After mixture has cooled, place in fridge for 3 hours.
9. Pour into your ice cream maker.
10. Mix 20-25 minutes or according to manufacturer's instructions.
11. Add cooled apples to the churning ice cream.
12. Churn for 5 more minutes.

CARAMEL APPLE ICE CREAM RECIPE

Custard Style

Prep Time: 35 minutes
Chill Time: 3 hours
Ice Cream Maker Time: Approximately 25-30 minutes
Makes: 1 ½ quarts
Servings: Ten ½ cup servings

Ingredients:
Apples
2 medium Granny Smith Apples
2 tbsp butter
2 tbsp sugar
1 tsp cinnamon
Ice Cream Base
2 eggs
1 cup granulated sugar
1 cup milk
2 cups heavy whipping cream

Directions:
Apples
1. Peel, core, and finely chop apples.
2. In a large saucepan, melt butter. Add apples and sugar to the saucepan. Stirring often, cook over medium-low to medium heat.
3. Cook approximately 15 minutes or until apples have softened.
4. Remove from heat and stir in cinnamon. Cool completely.

Ice Cream Base
1. Beat eggs until they are light and fluffy. Set aside.
2. In a large heavy saucepan (important! saucepan must be large!), heat sugar over medium heat, stirring constantly.
3. Continue to stir until sugar melts and turns into a golden brown liquid. Remove from heat.
4. Gradually and very carefully, pour milk into saucepan with sugar.
5. Be careful - the mixture will splatter and the sugar will turn hard.
6. Stir mixture over low heat until sugar melts and the mixture becomes smooth again. Pour in whipping cream and stir until well blended.
7. Pour some of this mixture over the eggs, mixing well.
8. Pour egg mixture back into saucepan and continue cooking over low heat until it thickens. Remove saucepan from heat and let cool.
9. Chill mixture in fridge for at least 3 hours.
10. Once chilled, pour in ice cream machine.
11. Churn 20-25 minutes or according to manufacturer's instructions.
12. Add cooled cinnamon apples and mix 5 more minutes.

CHERRY ICE CREAM RECIPE

Philadelphia Style

Prep Time: 15 minutes
Fridge: 2-24 hours
Ice Cream Maker Time: Approximately 25-30 minutes
Makes: 1 ½ quarts
Servings: Ten ½ cup servings

Ingredients:

2 cups fresh cherries, pits removed
¾ cup sugar
½ cup milk
2 cups heavy whipping cream
1 tsp vanilla extract

Directions:

1. In a food processor, process cherries and sugar together until smooth.
2. Place cherry mixture in the fridge for at least 2 hours. Leaving the cherries, in the fridge longer will enhance the flavor. Chilling for 24 hours will yield the best results.
3. Mix chilled cherries and milk together.
4. Stir in whipping cream and vanilla.
5. Pour mixture into ice cream maker.
6. Churn about 25-30 minutes or according to manufacturer's instructions.

Helpful Hint: You can also add about ¾ cup chocolate chips to the ice cream during the last 5 minutes of mixing.

CHERRY ICE CREAM RECIPE

Custard Style

Prep Time: 15 minutes
Chill Time: at least 3 hours
Ice Cream Maker Time: Approximately 25-30 minutes
Makes: 1 ½ quarts
Servings: Ten ½ cup servings

Ingredients:

Cherries
2 cups fresh cherries, pits removed
½ cup sugar

Ice Cream Base
2 eggs
¼ cup sugar
½ cup milk
2 cups heavy whipping cream
2 tsp vanilla extract

Directions:

Cherries

1. In food processor, process cherries and sugar together until smooth.
2. Place cherries in fridge for at least 2 hours. Leaving the cherries, in the fridge longer will enhance the flavor – 24 hours is best.

Ice Cream Base

1. Meanwhile, beat egg yolks with remaining ¼ cup sugar until the mixture is a pale yellow color.
2. Heat milk just to boiling in a saucepan and then pour the hot milk over the beaten eggs. Whisk together.
3. Pour this mixture back into the saucepan.
4. Stir milk/egg mixture over medium heat until mixture thickens and begins to stick to the back of your spoon.
5. Chill completely. This will take at least 3 hours.
6. Stir chilled cherries and chilled milk mixture together.
7. Add heavy cream and vanilla extract. Then combine well.
8. Pour into your ice cream maker.
9. Churn about 25-30 minutes or according to manufacturer's instructions.

Helpful Hint: You can also add about ¾ cup chocolate chips to the ice cream during the last 5 minutes of mixing.

CHOCOLATE CHERRY ICE CREAM RECIPE

Philadelphia Style

Prep Time: 25 minutes
Ice Cream Maker Time: Approximately 25-30 minutes
Makes: 1 ½ quarts
Servings: Ten ½ cup servings

Ingredients:
¾ cup granulated sugar
1 cup milk
2 cups heavy whipping cream
¼ cup shaved dark chocolate
¼ cup cherries, halved and pitted (fresh Bing cherries are best, if using canned – be sure to drain syrup)

Directions:

1. Dissolve sugar in milk with a whisk.
2. Add heavy whipping cream.
3. Pour this mixture into your ice cream maker.
4. Churn in ice cream maker about 20-25 minutes or according to manufacturer's instructions.
5. Add shaved dark chocolate and cherries to churning mixture.
6. Churn for an additional 5 minutes.

CHOCOLATE CHERRY ICE CREAM RECIPE

Custard Style

Prep Time: 25 minutes
Chill Time: 3 hours
Ice Cream Maker Time: Approximately 25-30 minutes
Makes: 1 ½ quarts
Servings: Ten ½ cup servings

Ingredients:

2 eggs
¾ cup granulated sugar
1 cup milk
2 cups whipping cream
¼ cup shaved dark chocolate
¼ cup cherries, halved and pitted (fresh Bing cherries are best, if using canned – be sure to drain syrup)

Directions:

1. Place eggs and sugar in a small bowl and beat well, until light and fluffy.
2. In a saucepan, heat milk until it starts to bubble.
3. Pour hot milk over beaten egg mixture. Stir well.
4. Pour this mixture back into saucepan and heat, stirring constantly until mixture becomes thick and sticks to the back of a spoon.
5. Chill for at least 3 hours.
6. After mixture is chilled, stir in whipping cream.
7. Pour this ice cream base into your ice cream machine.
8. Mix for 20-25 minutes (or according to manufacturer's instructions).
9. Into the churning ice cream, add dark chocolate and cherries.
10. Mix for 5 minutes.

LEMON ICE CREAM RECIPE

Philadelphia Style

Prep Time: 10 minutes
Ice Cream Maker Time: Approximately 25-30 minutes
Makes: 1 ½ quarts
Servings: Ten ½ cup servings

Ingredients:
1 cup milk
½ cup sugar
2 cups heavy whipping cream
½ cup lemon juice
2 tbsp freshly grated lemon peel (optional)

Directions:

1. Whisk milk and sugar together (about 1-2 minutes) until sugar completely dissolves.
2. Stir in whipping cream, lemon juice, and grated lemon peel until well-blended.
3. Pour immediately into ice cream maker (do not chill in fridge or lemon juice may curdle the milk).
4. Mix about 25-30 minutes or according to manufacturer's instructions.

LEMON ICE CREAM RECIPE

Custard Style

Prep Time: 25 minutes
Chill Time: 3 hours
Ice Cream Maker Time: Approximately 25-30 minutes
Makes: 1 ½ quarts
Servings: Ten ½ cup servings

Ingredients:
2 tbsp grated lemon peel
½ cup lemon juice
¾ cup sugar
4 egg yolks
Pinch of salt
1 cup milk
2 cups heavy cream

Directions:

1. Mix grated lemon peel and lemon juice together. Stir in sugar. Chill in fridge to enhance flavor.
2. Beat eggs with salt.
3. Heat milk in saucepan until it just begins to boil.
4. Pour hot milk over beaten eggs; mix well.
5. Pour milk mixture back into saucepan.
6. Heat. Stir constantly until mixture begins to stick to the back of your spoon and becomes thick. Don't let it boil!
7. Chill for at least 3 hours.
8. Stir in lemon mixture and heavy cream.
9. Pour into your ice cream maker.
10. Mix about 25-30 minutes or according to manufacturer's instructions.

MANGO ICE CREAM RECIPE

Philadelphia Style

Prep Time: 15 minutes
Chill Time: 1-24 hours
Ice Cream Maker Time: Approximately 25-30 minutes
Servings: Ten ½ cup servings
Makes: 1 ½ quarts

Ingredients:

Mango
1-2 ripe mangos
¼ cup sugar

Ice Cream Base
¾ cup milk
2/3 cup sugar
2 cups heavy cream
1 tsp vanilla extract

Directions:

Mango
1. Puree mango.
2. Combine mango and ¼ cup sugar in a small, airtight container.
3. Chill mango mixture in the fridge for at least 1 hour. It's best to let it sit in the fridge for 12-24 hours – this will enhance the flavor – do whatever you have time for.

Ice Cream Base
1. Mix milk and sugar together so that the sugar dissolves (this will take about 1 -2 minutes with a hand mixer or whisk).
2. Add about 1 to 1 ½ cups of puree to the milk mixture, stirring well.
3. Stir in cream and vanilla extract.
4. Pour into ice cream maker.
5. Mix about 25-30 minutes or according to manufacturer's instructions.

MANGO ICE CREAM RECIPE

Custard Style

Prep Time: 15 minutes
Chill Time: 3-24 hours
Ice Cream Maker Time: Approximately 25-30 minutes
Makes: 1 ½ quarts
Servings: Ten ½ cup servings

Ingredients:

Mango
1-2 ripe mangos
¼ cup sugar

Ice Cream Base
2 eggs
¾ cup sugar
¾ cup milk
2 cups heavy cream
1 tsp vanilla extract

Directions:

Mango
1. Puree mango.
2. In a small, airtight container, mix together mango and ¼ cup sugar.
3. In the refrigerator, chill mango puree for at least 1 hour (chilling 12-24 hours will enhance your ice cream's flavor).

Ice Cream Base
1. Beat eggs until they are light and fluffy (1-2 min).
2. Slowly add sugar to the eggs and beat for 1 more minute.
3. In a saucepan, heat milk until it just begins to boil.
4. Pour hot milk over beaten eggs, stirring to combine.
5. Pour mixture back into the saucepan and heat, stirring constantly (don't let mixture boil).
6. Remove from heat when mixture thickens and begins to stick to your spoon. Chill at least 3 hours until cooled completely.
7. Add mango puree to milk mixture. Stir in cream and vanilla.
8. Pour into ice cream maker.
9. Mix about 25-30 minutes or according to manufacturer's instructions.

ORANGE ICE CREAM RECIPE

Philadelphia Style

Prep Time: 15 minutes
Ice Cream Maker Time: Approximately 25 minutes
Makes: 1 ½ quarts
Servings: Ten ½ cup servings

Ingredients:
1 ½ cups heavy whipping cream
1 ½ cups freshly squeezed orange juice (or just plain orange juice works fine too!)
1/3 cup sugar (or more if you'd like!)
1 tbsp lemon juice
1 tbsp orange zest (if you want - gives the ice cream a classy look and taste)
1 tsp pure vanilla extract
½ cup shaved chocolate (optional)

Directions:

1. Combine all ingredients in a large bowl, stirring until mixed and sugar is dissolved.
2. For best results, cover and place in the fridge until it is cold (several hours or overnight). This will help your ice cream to have a better texture.
3. Pour the ice cream mixture to your ice cream machine and mix according to the manufacturer's instructions.
4. Churn about 25 minutes or according to manufacturer's instructions.
5. Add shaved chocolate during the last 5 minutes of mixing, if desired.

ORANGE ICE CREAM RECIPE

Custard Style

Prep Time: 10 minutes
Chill: 3 hours
Ice Cream Maker Time: Approximately 25 minutes
Makes: 1 ½ quarts
Servings: Ten ½ cup servings

Ingredients:
2 large eggs
1/3 cup granulated sugar
1 ½ cups heavy whipping cream
1 ½ cups freshly squeezed orange juice (or just plain orange juice works fine too!)
1 tbsp lemon juice
1 tbsp orange zest (if you want – gives the ice cream a classy look and taste)
1 tsp pure vanilla extract
½ cup shaved chocolate (optional)

Directions:

1. Whisk eggs for 1-2 minutes until they are light and fluffy.
2. Gradually, whisk in sugar, then whisk for 1 minute more.
3. Heat whipping cream in saucepan until it just begins to bubble.
4. Pour over beaten eggs, then return to saucepan.
5. Continue to heat over low heat until mixture begins to thicken and stick to the back of your spoon.
6. Remove from heat and chill in fridge – about 3 hours.
7. Add orange juice, lemon juice, orange zest, and vanilla, stirring until completely blended.
8. Pour this mixture into your ice cream maker.
9. Mix about 25 minutes or according to manufacturer's directions.
10. Add shaved chocolate during the last 5 minutes of mixing, if desired.

PEACH ICE CREAM RECIPE

Philadelphia Style

Prep Time: 15 minutes
Chill Time: 2 hours
Ice Cream Maker Time: Approximately 25-30 minutes
Makes: 1 ½ quarts
Servings: Ten ½ cup servings

Ingredients:

Peaches
4 ripe peaches
½ cup lemon juice
½ cup granulated sugar

Ice Cream Base
1 cup milk
¾ cup sugar
2 cups heavy whipping cream

Directions:

Peaches
1. Wash peaches well.
2. You can leave the skin on or take it off – whichever you prefer.
3. Finely chop or mash peaches.
4. Combine peaches, lemon juice, and ½ cup sugar in a small, airtight container.
5. Chill peach mixture in the fridge for at least 2 hours.

Ice Cream Base
1. Mix milk and sugar together, dissolving the sugar.
2. Strain peaches and add juice to milk mixture, setting peaches aside.
3. Stir in heavy cream.
4. Pour into ice cream maker.
5. Mix about 20-25 minutes or according to manufacturer's instructions.
6. Add peaches to the churning ice cream.
7. Mix 5 more minutes in your ice cream maker.

PEACH ICE CREAM RECIPE

Custard Style

Prep Time: 15 minutes
Chill Time: 3 hours
Ice Cream Maker Time: Approximately 25-30 minutes
Makes: 1 ½ quarts
Servings: Ten ½ cup servings

Ingredients:
Peaches
4 ripe peaches
½ cup lemon juice
½ cup granulated sugar

Ice Cream Base
2 eggs
1 cup milk
¾ cup sugar
2 cups heavy whipping cream

Directions:
Peaches
1. Wash peaches well (leave the skin on or take it off – whichever you prefer). Finely chop or mash peaches.
2. Combine peaches, lemon juice, and ½ cup sugar in a small, airtight container. Chill peach mixture in the fridge for at least 2 hours.

Ice Cream Base
1. Beat eggs about 1-2 min until they are light and fluffy.
2. Slowly add sugar to the eggs and beat for 1 more minute.
3. Heat milk in a saucepan just until it begins to bubble.
4. Pour over beaten eggs and return to saucepan. Continue to heat over low heat until mixture begins to stick to back of spoon.
5. Remove from heat and chill about 3 hours.
6. Strain peaches and add the peach juice to milk mixture, setting peaches aside.
7. Stir in heavy cream.
8. Pour the ice cream base into your ice cream maker.
9. Mix about 20-25 minutes or according to manufacturer's instructions.
10. Add peaches to the ice cream as it mixes.
11. Mix 5 more minutes in your ice cream maker.

PINA COLADA ICE CREAM RECIPE

Philadelphia Style

Prep Time: 15 minutes
Ice Cream Maker Time: Approximately 20-25 minutes
Makes: 1 ½ quarts
Servings: Ten ½ cup servings

Ingredients:

1 cup coconut milk
½ cup sugar
1 ½ cups whipping cream
½ cup crushed pineapple

Directions:

1. Mix the sugar and the coconut together with a whisk or a fork until the sugar completely dissolves.
2. Stir in the heavy whipping cream.
3. Add the crushed pineapple and combine well.
4. Pour the pineapple coconut mixture into your ice cream maker.
5. Churn about 20-25 minutes or according to manufacturer's instructions.

PINA COLADA ICE CREAM RECIPE

Custard Style

Prep Time: 15 minutes
Chill Time: at least 3 hours
Ice Cream Maker Time: Approximately 25-30 minutes
Makes: 1 ½ quarts
Servings: Ten ½ cup servings

Ingredients:
1 cup coconut milk
½ cup sugar
2 egg yolks, lightly beaten
1 ½ cups whipping cream
½ cup crushed pineapple

Directions:

1. In a saucepan, combine coconut milk and sugar.
2. Warm over medium heat just until it begins to bubble.
3. In a bowl, beat the egg yolks.
4. Pour the heated coconut milk mixture over the beaten egg yolks. Stir well.
5. Pour mixture back into the saucepan.
6. While stirring constantly, heat mixture over medium-low heat until it becomes thick (it will start to stick to the back of your spoon).
7. Place in fridge until completely chilled (about 3 hours).
8. Once cooled, add the whipping cream and crushed pineapple.
9. Pour into ice cream maker and churn about 20-25 minutes or according to manufacturer's instructions.

PINEAPPLE ICE CREAM RECIPE

Philadelphia Style

Prep Time: 15 minutes
Fridge: 2 - 24 hours
Ice Cream Maker Time: Approximately 25-30 minutes
Makes: 1 ½ quarts
Servings: Ten ½ cup servings

Ingredients:

Pineapple
½ fresh pineapple (about 2 cups) (or you can used canned)
½ cup sugar
½ lime (optional)

Ice Cream Base
½ cup sugar
½ cup milk
2 cups heavy whipping cream

Directions:

Pineapple
1. Place pineapple, sugar, and the lime (if you're using it) in a food processor or blender and blend until completely smooth.
2. Place pineapple mixture in the fridge for at least 2 hours. Leaving the fresh pineapple, in the fridge longer will enhance the flavor, so I kept mine in the fridge overnight.

Ice Cream
1. Whisk milk and sugar together until sugar dissolves.
2. Add whipping cream and combine well.
3. Stir in chilled pineapple mixture.
4. Pour into your ice cream maker.
5. Churn about 25-30 minutes or according to manufacturer's instructions.

PINEAPPLE ICE CREAM RECIPE

Custard Style

Prep Time: 15 minutes
Chill Time: at least 3 hours
Ice Cream Maker Time: Approximately 25-30 minutes
Makes: 1 ½ quarts
Servings: Ten ½ cup servings

Ingredients:
Pineapple
½ fresh pineapple (about 2 cups) (or you can used canned)
½ cup sugar
½ lime (optional)

Ice Cream Base
½ cup sugar
3 large eggs
½ cup milk
2 cups heavy whipping cream

Directions:

Pineapple
1. Place pineapple and sugar in a blender or food processor.
2. Add lime, if desired.
3. Process mixture until smooth and becomes watery syrup.
4. Chill pineapple mixture in the fridge for at least 2 hours for flavors to blend. Leaving the pineapple in the fridge longer will enhance the flavor. I chilled mine overnight.

Ice Cream Base
1. While the pineapple mixture is chilling, beat eggs with remaining ½ cup sugar until the mixture is pale yellow.
2. Heat milk over medium heat, just until bubbles start to form around the edges. Pour the hot milk from the saucepan over the beaten eggs, then whisk lightly.
3. Pour this mixture back into the saucepan and continue to heat over medium heat. While stirring, continue to heat mixture until it thickens and starts to stick to the back of your spoon.
4. Chill completely – this will take at least 3 hours.
5. Add whipping cream to chilled milk mixture and combine.
6. Stir in chilled pineapple mixture.
7. Pour into your ice cream machine and churn about 25-30 minutes or according to manufacturer's instructions.

PUMPKIN ICE CREAM RECIPE

Philadelphia Style

Prep Time: 15 minutes
Chill Time: 30 min
Ice Cream Maker Time: Approximately 25-30 minutes
Makes: 1 ½ quarts
Servings: Ten ½ cup servings

Ingredients:

15 oz can pumpkin puree (1 ¾ cup)
¾ cup brown sugar
1 ½ tsp cinnamon
½ tsp ground ginger
¼ tsp nutmeg
Pinch of ground cloves
2 cups heavy whipping cream

Directions:

1. In a large bowl, mix pumpkin puree, brown sugar, and spices together.
2. Stir in heavy whipping cream.
3. Chill in fridge for at least 30 minutes.
4. Pour into ice cream maker and mix about 25-30 minutes or according to manufacturer's instructions.

Pumpkin Pie Ice Cream Recipe: If you'd like to turn this ice cream into Pumpkin Pie ice cream, just add ½ - ¾ cup of broken graham crackers to the ice cream during the last 5 minutes of mixing.

PUMPKIN ICE CREAM RECIPE

Custard Style

Prep Time: 15 minutes
Chill Time: 3hours
Ice Cream Maker Time: Approximately 25-30 minutes
Makes: 1 ½ quart
Servings: Ten ½ cup servings

Ingredients:

15 oz can pumpkin puree (1 ¾ cup)
1 ½ tsp cinnamon
½ tsp ground ginger
¼ tsp nutmeg
Pinch of ground cloves
5 egg yolks
¾ cup brown sugar, divided
2 cups heavy whipping cream

Directions:

1. In a large bowl, mix pumpkin puree and spices together well. Place in refrigerator.
2. Beat egg yolks and ¼ cup brown sugar together in a bowl.
3. In a large saucepan, heat heavy whipping cream and ½ cup brown sugar until it just begins to bubble.
4. Pour hot cream mixture over beaten eggs. Mix well.
5. Return to saucepan and heat over medium heat, stirring constantly until mixture begins to coat the back of your spoon.
6. Cool. Stir in pumpkin mixture.
7. Chill in fridge for at least 3 hours.
8. Pour into ice cream maker and mix about 25-30 minutes or according to manufacturer's instructions.

Pumpkin Pie Ice Cream Recipe: If you'd like to turn this ice cream into Pumpkin Pie ice cream, just add ½ - ¾ cup of broken graham crackers to the ice cream during the last 5 minutes of mixing.

RASPBERRY ICE CREAM RECIPE

Philadelphia Style

Prep Time: 15 minutes
Fridge: 2 - 24 hours
Ice Cream Maker Time: Approximately 25-30 minutes
Makes: 1 ½ quarts
Servings: Ten ½ cup servings

Ingredients:
1 pint (2 cups) raspberries (fresh or frozen)
1 cup sugar
1 cup milk
2 cups heavy whipping cream
2 tsp vanilla extract

Directions:

1. Lightly mash raspberries.
2. Mix raspberries and sugar together.
3. Place raspberry mixture in the fridge for at least 2 hours. Leaving the raspberries, in the fridge longer will enhance the flavor. I refrigerated mine for about 24 hours.
4. Mix raspberries and milk together.
5. Add whipping cream and vanilla. Combine thoroughly.
6. Pour mixture into ice cream maker.
7. Churn about 25-30 minutes or according to manufacturer's instructions.

RASPBERRY ICE CREAM RECIPE

Custard Style

Prep Time: 15 minutes
Chill Time: at least 3 hours
Ice Cream Maker Time: Approximately 25-30 minutes
Makes: 1 ½ quarts
Servings: Ten ½ cup servings

Ingredients:
1 pint (2 cups) raspberries (fresh or frozen)
¾ cup sugar
2 eggs
1/3 cup sugar
1 cup milk
2 cups heavy whipping cream
2 tsp vanilla extract

Directions:

1. Lightly mash raspberries.
2. Combine raspberries and ¾ cup sugar. Mix together well.
3. Place raspberry mixture in the fridge for at least 2 hours. Leaving the raspberries, in the fridge longer will enhance the flavor. I refrigerated mine for about 24 hours.
4. Meanwhile, beat egg yolks with remaining 1/3 cup sugar until the mixture is a pale yellow color.
5. Heat milk just to boiling in a saucepan.
6. Pour the hot milk over the beaten eggs.
7. Pour this mixture into the saucepan.
8. Stir milk/egg mixture over medium heat until mixture thickens and begins to stick to the back of your spoon.
9. Chill completely – at least 3 hours.
10. Stir chilled raspberries and chilled milk mixture together.
11. Add whipping cream and vanilla extract. Combine well.
12. Pour this ice cream base into your ice cream maker.
13. Churn about 25-30 minutes or according to manufacturer's instructions.

STRAWBERRY ICE CREAM RECIPE

Philadelphia Style

Prep Time: 12 minutes
Chill Time: 2 - 24 hours
Ice Cream Maker Time: Approximately 25-30 minutes
Makes: 1 ½ quarts
Servings: Ten ½ cup servings

Ingredients:

Strawberries
16 oz fresh strawberries (1 pint)
3 tbsp lemon juice
1/3 cup sugar

Ice Cream Base
1 cup milk
2/3 cup granulated sugar
2 cups heavy cream
1 tsp vanilla extract

Directions:

Strawberries
1. Wash, stem, and slice strawberries.
2. Combine strawberries, lemon juice, and 1/3 cup sugar in a small airtight container.
3. Place strawberry mixture in the fridge for at least 2 hours. Leaving the strawberries, in the fridge longer will enhance the flavor.

Ice Cream Base
1. Mix milk and sugar, allowing the sugar to dissolve (mix about 1-2 minutes with a hand mixer or whisk).
2. Drain strawberries, adding juice to milk mixture. Set strawberries aside.
3. Stir in heavy cream and vanilla.
4. Pour mixture into your ice cream maker.
5. Mix about 20-25 minutes.
6. Add about half the strawberries to ice cream mixture (use the other half as a fresh berry topping!).
7. Mix 5 minutes more in your ice cream maker.

STRAWBERRY ICE CREAM RECIPE

Custard Style

Prep Time: 15 minutes
Fridge: 2 – 24 hours
Chill Time: 3 hours
Ice Cream Maker Time: Approximately 25-30 minutes
Makes: 1 ½ quarts
Servings: Ten ½ cup servings

Ingredients:
16 oz fresh strawberries (1 pint)
3 tbsp lemon juice
1/3 cup sugar

2 eggs
1 cup milk
2/3 cup granulated sugar
2 cups heavy cream
1 tsp vanilla extract

Directions:

1. Wash, stem, and slice strawberries.
2. Combine strawberries, lemon juice, and 1/3 cup sugar in a small airtight container.
3. Place strawberry mixture in the fridge for at least 2 hours. Leaving the strawberries, in the fridge longer will enhance the flavor.
4. Meanwhile, beat egg yolks with remaining 2/3 cup sugar until the mixture is a pale yellow color.
5. Heat milk just to boiling in a saucepan.
6. Pour the hot milk over the beaten eggs.
7. Pour this mixture into the saucepan.
8. Stir milk/egg mixture over medium heat until mixture thickens and begins to stick to the back of your spoon.
9. Chill completely – at least 3 hours.
10. Stir chilled strawberries and chilled milk mixture together.
11. Add whipping cream and vanilla extract. Combine well.
12. Pour this ice cream base into your ice cream maker.
13. Churn about 25-30 minutes or according to manufacturer's instructions.

WATERMELON ICE CREAM RECIPE

Philadelphia Style

Prep Time: 15 minutes
Chill Time: 3-24 hours
Ice Cream Maker Time: Approximately 25-30 minutes
Makes: 1 ½ quarts
Servings: Ten ½ cup servings

Ingredients:
Watermelon
2 ½ - 3 cups chopped watermelon
¼ cup sugar

Ice Cream Base
½ cup milk
½ cup granulated sugar
2 cups heavy cream
1 tsp vanilla extract
¼ tsp salt (optional, improves texture, brings out taste)
1 envelope gelatin (optional, improves texture)
½ chocolate chips (optional, for "watermelon seeds")

Directions:
Watermelon
1. Puree watermelon in a bowl and add ¼ cup sugar.
2. Pour 1 ½ cups of watermelon puree into a small saucepan and heat over medium-low heat.
3. Bring watermelon puree to a boil and boil for several minutes.
4. Chill watermelon mixture in the fridge until completely cooled, about 3 hours. Storing in refrigerator 12-24 hours will strengthen the flavor.

Ice Cream Base
1. With a hand mixer or whisk, mix milk and sugar together so that the sugar dissolves.
2. Add cooled watermelon puree to the milk mixture.
3. Stir in cream, vanilla, salt, and sprinkle in gelatin – make sure gelatin dissolves completely.
4. Pour into ice cream maker.
5. Mix about 20-25 minutes.
6. Add chocolate chips to churning ice cream.
7. Mix 5 more minutes in your ice cream maker.

WATERMELON ICE CREAM RECIPE

Custard Style

Prep Time: 15 minutes
Chill Time: 3-24 hours
Ice Cream Maker Time: Approximately 25-30 minutes
Makes: 1 ½ quarts
Servings: Ten ½ cup servings

Ingredients:
Watermelon
2 ½ - 3 cups chopped watermelon
¼ cup sugar
Ice Cream Base
2 eggs
½ cup granulated sugar
½ cup milk
2 cups heavy cream
1 tsp vanilla extract
¼ tsp salt (optional, improves texture, brings out taste)
1 envelope gelatin (optional, improves texture)
½ chocolate chips (optional, for "watermelon seeds")

Directions:
Watermelon
1. Puree watermelon well. Stir in ¼ cup sugar.
2. Pour 1 ½ cups watermelon puree into a saucepan and heat over med-low heat. Bring watermelon to a boil and boil for several min.
3. Remove from heat and chill until completely cooled, about 3 hours. Chilling for 12-24 hours will enhance the flavor.

Ice Cream Base
1. Beat eggs until they are light and fluffy (1-2 min).
2. Add sugar slowly to the eggs and then beat this for 1 minute more.
3. In a saucepan, heat milk until it just begins to boil.
4. Pour hot milk over beaten eggs and then stir to combine.
5. Stirring constantly, pour this mixture back into the saucepan and heat – but do not let the mixture boil.
6. When the mixture thickens and begins to stick to the back of your spoon, remove from heat.
7. Chill at least 3 hours until cooled completely.
8. Add cooled watermelon to the milk mixture. Stir in cream and vanilla, adding salt and gelatin if desired.
9. Pour into ice cream maker. Mix about 20-25 minutes.
10. Add chocolate chips to ice cream mixture, if desired.
11. Mix 5 more minutes in your ice cream machine.

67

Sugar n' Spice Recipes

BASIL ICE CREAM RECIPE

Philadelphia Style

Prep Time: 15 minutes
Chill: 5 hours
Ice Cream Maker Time: Approximately 25-30 minutes
Makes: 1 ½ quarts
Servings: Ten ½ cup servings

Ingredients:
1 cup milk
1 cup sugar
1 ½ cup fresh basil
2 cups heavy whipping cream
1 tsp vanilla extract

Directions:

1. In a saucepan, stir milk and sugar together.
2. Heat milk mixture to boiling.
3. Stir in fresh basil leaves and remove from heat.
4. Cover and let basil and milk mixture stand for 15-20 minutes.
5. In a blender or with a stick blender, process basil and milk mixture until it becomes smooth.
6. Pour mixture through strainer.
7. Stir in whipping cream and vanilla extract.
8. Chill until completely cooled, about 5 hours.
9. Pour mixture into ice cream maker.
10. Churn about 25-30 minutes or according to manufacturer's instructions.

BASIL ICE CREAM RECIPE

Custard Style

Prep Time: 15 minutes
Chill Time: at least 5 hours
Ice Cream Maker Time: Approximately 25-30 minutes
Makes: 1 ½ quarts
Servings: Ten ½ cup servings

Ingredients:

1 cup milk
1 cup sugar, divided
1 ½ cup fresh basil leaves
7 egg yolks
2 cups heavy whipping cream
1 tsp vanilla

Directions:

1. In a saucepan, heat milk to boiling.
2. Stir in fresh basil leaves and remove from heat.
3. Cover and allow this mixture to sit for 15-20 minutes.
4. In a blender or with a stick blender, process basil mixture until smooth.
5. Pour mixture through a strainer to remove excess solids.
6. In another saucepan over medium heat, heat whipping cream and ½ cup sugar, cook until bubbly.
7. Beat egg yolks with remaining ½ cup sugar until the mixture is a pale yellow color.
8. Pour about a quarter of the hot whipping cream mixture into the beaten egg yolks.
9. Stir in basil mixture and vanilla.
10. Heat this mixture in the saucepan with the rest of the heated whipping cream.
11. Stir over medium heat until mixture thickens and begins to stick to the back of your spoon.
12. Chill completely – at least 5 hours.
13. Pour into your ice cream maker.
14. Churn about 25-30 minutes or according to manufacturer's instructions.

CINNAMON ICE CREAM RECIPE

Philadelphia Style

Prep Time: 7 minutes
Ice Cream Maker Time: Approximately 20-25 minutes
Makes: 1 ½ quarts
Servings: Ten ½ cup servings

Ingredients:
1 cup milk
½ cup sugar
2 cups heavy whipping cream
1 tsp vanilla extract
2 tsp cinnamon

Directions:

1. Mix milk and sugar together using a wire whisk or hand mixer so that the sugar completely dissolves.
2. Stir in heavy cream, vanilla, and cinnamon, making sure that the cinnamon is well blended throughout.
3. Pour mixture into your ice cream maker.
4. Mix about 20-25 minutes.

Helpful Hint: Cinnamon has a tendency to sink to the bottom of the ice cream mixture, so make sure that the ice cream is freshly stirred before pouring it in the ice cream maker!

CINNAMON ICE CREAM RECIPE

Custom Style

Prep Time: 10 minutes
Chill Time: 3 hours
Ice Cream Maker Time: Approximately 20-25 minutes
Makes: 1 ½ quarts
Servings: Ten ½ cup servings

Ingredients:

2 large eggs
½ cup sugar
1 cup milk
2 cups heavy whipping cream
1 tsp vanilla extract
2 tsp cinnamon

Directions:

1. Whisk eggs until they are light and fluffy (1 to 2 minutes).
2. Gradually, stir in sugar, then whisk for 1 minute.
3. In a saucepan, heat milk until it just starts to bubble around the edges, but don't let it boil.
4. Pour milk over beaten eggs and mix well.
5. Return to saucepan.
6. Heat over low heat, stirring constantly until mixture thickens and begins to stick to the back of your spoon.
7. Remove from heat and chill in fridge until completely cool – about 3 hours.
8. Add heavy cream, vanilla, and cinnamon.
9. Stir until completely blended, making sure the cinnamon is mixed throughout.
10. Pour into ice cream maker.
11. Mix about 20-25 minutes or according to manufacturer's directions.

Helpful Hint: Since cinnamon will settle at the bottom of the ice cream mixture, be sure to stir the ice cream before pouring it into your ice cream machine!

GINGER ICE CREAM RECIPE

Philadelphia Style

Prep Time: 10 minutes
Ice Cream Maker Time: Approximately 25-30 minutes
Makes: 1 ½ quarts
Servings: Ten ½ cup servings

Ingredients:
1 cup milk
½ cup brown sugar
¼ cup granulated sugar
2 cups heavy whipping cream
1 tsp vanilla extract
½ tsp ground ginger

Directions:

1. Whisk milk and sugar together (about 1-2 minutes) until sugar completely dissolves.
2. Stir in heavy whipping cream, vanilla, and ginger until mixed well.
3. Pour into your ice cream maker.
4. Mix about 25-30 minutes or according to manufacturer's instructions.

GINGER ICE CREAM RECIPE

Custard Style

Prep Time: 25 minutes
Chill Time: 3 hours
Ice Cream Maker Time: Approximately 25-30 minutes
Makes: 1 ½ quarts
Servings: Ten ½ cup servings

Ingredients:
2 eggs
½ cup brown sugar
¼ cup granulated sugar
1 cup milk
2 cups heavy cream
½ tsp ground ginger

Directions:

1. Beat eggs with sugar.
2. Heat milk in saucepan until it just begins to bubble around the edges.
3. Pour hot milk over egg mixture, stirring well.
4. Pour milk/egg mixture back into saucepan and heat on low.
5. Stir constantly until mixture thickens and begins to stick to the back of your spoon. Don't let it boil though!
6. Chill for at least 3 hours.
7. Stir in heavy cream and ground ginger.
8. Pour ice cream base into your ice cream maker.
9. Mix about 25-30 minutes or according to manufacturer's instructions.

HONEY ICE CREAM RECIPE

Philadelphia Style

Prep Time: 7 minutes
Ice Cream Maker Time: Approximately 20-25 minutes
Makes: 1 ½ quarts
Servings: Ten ½ cup servings

Ingredients:
1 cup milk
½ cup honey
2 cups heavy whipping cream
1 tsp vanilla extract

Directions:

1. Mix honey and milk together using a wire whisk to completely dissolve the honey.
2. Stir in heavy cream and vanilla.
3. Pour mixture into your ice cream maker.
4. Mix about 20-25 minutes or according to manufacturer's instructions.

HONEY ICE CREAM RECIPE

Custard Style

Prep Time: 7 minutes
Chill Time: at least 3 hours
Ice Cream Maker Time: Approximately 20-25 minutes
Makes: 1 ½ quarts
Servings: Ten ½ cup servings

Ingredients:
4 egg yolks
2/3 cup honey
1 cup milk
2 cups heavy whipping cream
1 tsp vanilla extract

Directions:

1. Whisk eggs until they are light and fluffy.
2. Slowly stir in honey and whisk until well blended.
3. In a saucepan, bring milk to a slow boil.
4. Pour hot milk over egg mixture and combine.
5. Pour mixture back into saucepan and heat over low heat, stirring constantly until mixture begins to thicken and stick to the back of your spoon.
6. Cool and then chill in fridge for at least 3 hours.
7. Stir heavy cream and vanilla into cooled milk mixture.
8. Pour into ice cream maker and mix about 20-25 minutes or according to manufacturer's instructions.

SEA SALT ICE CREAM RECIPE

Philadelphia Style

Prep Time: 15 minutes
Ice Cream Maker Time: Approximately 25-30 minutes
Makes: 1 ½ quarts
Servings: Ten ½ cup servings

Ingredients:
1 cup milk
2/3 cup sugar
2 cups heavy whipping cream
1 ½ tsp sea salt***

Directions:

1. Mix milk and sugar until the sugar dissolves completely. You can use a wire whisk or hand mixer if you want.
2. Add the heavy whipping cream and the sea salt to taste.
3. Stir well so salt dissolves.
4. Pour mixture into ice cream maker.
5. Churn this ice cream mixture about 25-30 minutes or according to manufacturer's instructions.

***Helpful Hints:** Different sea salts vary in saltiness from other types of sea salts. I used French Grey Sea Salt. Some prefer a more salty flavor and others prefer just a hint of saltiness. Add sea salt according to your taste preference.

Also keep in mind that the salt needs to dissolve completely into the ice cream mixture to affect the taste. Stir and give the sea salt a chance to dissolve and permeate the mixture before adding more.

SEA SALT ICE CREAM RECIPE

Custard Style

Prep Time: 15 minutes
Chill Time: at least 3 hours
Ice Cream Maker Time: Approximately 25-30 minutes
Makes: 1 ½ quarts
Servings: Ten ½ cup servings

Ingredients:
2/3 cup sugar
4 egg yolks
1 cup milk
2 cups heavy whipping cream
1 ½ tsp sea salt***

Directions:

1. Beat eggs and sugar together, continuing to beat until the mixture is a soft yellow color and become thick.
2. Heat the milk to a low simmer.
3. Slowly add the hot milk to the egg and sugar mixture.
4. Pour this new mixture back into the pan and heat on low.
5. Stir constantly until the mixture begins to thicken and starts to coat the back of the spoon – being careful not to boil.
6. Remove from heat and cool completely in the refrigerator about 2 hours or more.
7. Add sea salt and whipping cream.
8. Churn in ice cream maker according to manufacturer's instructions - about 25-30 min.

***Helpful Hints:** There are many different types of sea salts. Each type of sea salt varies in saltiness from the other types. When I made this recipe, I used French Grey Sea Salt. Also keep in mind that everyone's preferences are different, you may prefer a more salty flavor or you may prefer a less salty one. Add sea salt according to your taste preference.

It's also a good idea to remember that the salt needs to dissolve completely to affect the taste. Allow the sea salt to dissolve and permeate the ice cream base before adding more.

Nutty Recipes

BUTTER PECAN ICE CREAM RECIPE

Philadelphia Style

Prep Time: 15 minutes
Ice Cream Maker Time: Approximately 20-25 minutes
Makes: 1 ½ quarts
Servings: Ten ½ cup servings

Ingredients:
½ cup butter
1 cup chopped pecans
1 cup milk
½ cup brown sugar
2 cups heavy whipping cream
1 ½ tsp vanilla extract

Directions:

1. In a saucepan, melt butter over low heat.
2. Mix in chopped pecans, stirring until pecans start to brown.
3. Strain mixture, placing butter in one dish and pecans in another.
4. Cool butter and pecans completely.
5. In a separate bowl, mix milk and sugar together until the sugar dissolves (about 1-2 minutes).
6. Stir in cream and vanilla and cooled melted butter.
7. Pour mixture into ice cream maker.
8. Mix about 15-20 minutes or according to manufacturer's instructions.
9. Add cooled buttered pecans to ice cream.
10. Churn for 5 additional minutes.

BUTTER PECAN ICE CREAM RECIPE

Custard Style

Prep Time: 15 minutes
Chill Time: at least 2 hours
Ice Cream Maker Time: Approximately 20-25 minutes
Makes: 1 ½ quarts
Servings: Ten ½ cup servings

Ingredients:
2 large eggs
2/3 cup brown sugar
1 cup milk
½ cup butter
1 cup chopped pecans
2 cups heavy whipping cream
1 tsp vanilla extract

Directions:

1. Whisk eggs about 1-2 minutes until light and fluffy.
2. Slowly whisk in sugar until completely blended and then whisk 1 more minute.
3. In a saucepan, heat milk until it just begins to bubble.
4. Pour hot milk into egg mixture and blend well.
5. Pour mixture back into saucepan and heat over low heat, stirring constantly until mixture thickens and starts to stick to your spoon.
6. Chill about 2 hours.
7. Meanwhile, in a saucepan, melt butter over low heat.
8. Add pecans, stirring until pecans start to brown.
9. Strain. Place pecans and butter in separate bowls.
10. Cool pecans and butter completely.
11. Once milk mixture has cooled, stir in heavy cream, vanilla, and cooled melted butter. Blend well.
12. Pour into your ice cream maker.
13. Mix about 15-20 minutes or according to manufacturer's instructions.
14. Add cooled buttered pecans to churning ice cream.
15. Mix for 5 more minutes.

COCONUT ICE CREAM RECIPE

Philadelphia Style

Prep Time: 15 minutes
Ice Cream Maker Time: Approximately 20-25 minutes
Makes: 1 ½ arts
Servings: Ten ½ cup servings

Ingredients:
1 cup coconut milk
1/3 cup sugar
2 cups heavy whipping cream
1 teaspoon vanilla

Directions:

1. Stir the sugar and the coconut together until sugar dissolves completely.
2. Stir in the heavy whipping cream and the vanilla.
3. Pour this coconut mixture into your ice cream maker.
4. Churn about 20-25 minutes or according to manufacturer's instructions.

COCONUT ICE CREAM RECIPE

Custard Style

Prep Time: 15 minutes
Chill Time: at least 3 hours
Ice Cream Maker Time: Approximately 20-25 minutes
Makes: 1 ½ quarts
Servings: Ten ½ cup servings

Ingredients:

1 cup coconut milk
1/3 cup sugar
2 egg yolks, lightly beaten
2 cups whipping cream
1 teaspoon vanilla

Directions:

1. Stir coconut milk and sugar together in a saucepan.
2. Over medium heat, warm this mixture until it begins to bubble.
3. Beat egg yolks.
4. Pour the coconut milk mixture over the egg yolks and whisk.
5. Pour this back into the saucepan.
6. While stirring constantly, heat mixture over low-medium heat until it thickens and begins to stick to the back of your spoon.
7. Place in your refrigerator until chilled (about 3 hours).
8. Stir in the whipping cream and vanilla.
9. Churn in your ice cream machine about 20-25 minutes or according to manufacturer's instructions.

THAI COCONUT ICE CREAM RECIPE

Philadelphia Style

Prep Time: 15 minutes
Chill Time: at least 3 hours
Ice Cream Maker Time: Approximately 25-30 minutes
Makes: 1 ½ quarts
Servings: Ten ½ cup servings

Ingredients:
5 cups coconut milk (about three 13.5 oz cans)
1 ½ cups sugar
¾ tsp salt

Directions:

1. In a saucepan, mix all ingredients (coconut milk, sugar, and salt).
2. Heat over medium heat until mixture begins to boil. Make sure you stir constantly.
3. Allow the mixture to simmer for approximately 4 minutes. The sugar should be completely dissolved.
4. Remove the coconut milk mixture from the heat and pour into a different bowl to let it cool.
5. *Tip:* To prevent, the coconut milk from forming a skin on the top, lay a piece of plastic wrap along the surface.
6. Let the mixture cool completely. This will take at least 3 hours or you can chill it overnight.
7. Pour the cooled mixture into your ice cream maker.
8. Churn for 25-30 minutes or according to manufacturer's instructions.

TOASTED COCONUT ICE CREAM RECIPE

Philadelphia Style

Prep Time: 15 minutes
Ice Cream Maker Time: Approximately 25-30 minutes
Makes: 1 ½ quarts
Servings: Ten ½ cup servings

Ingredients:

½ cup coconut flakes
2 tablespoons butter
1 cup coconut milk
1/3 cup sugar
2 cups heavy whipping cream
1 teaspoon vanilla

Directions:

1. Put coconut flakes and butter in a small saucepan.
2. Over medium-low heat, toast coconut in butter, stirring frequently until coconut becomes slightly browned.
3. Cool completely.
4. In a medium bowl, stir sugar and coconut milk together until sugar is completely dissolved.
5. Add heavy whipping cream and vanilla.
6. Pour this coconut ice cream base into your ice cream machine.
7. Churn about 20-25 minutes or according to manufacturer's instructions.
8. Add cooled toasted coconut to the churning ice cream and churn an additional 5 minutes.

TOASTED COCONUT ICE CREAM RECIPE

Custard Style

Prep Time: 15 minutes
Chill Time: at least 3 hours
Ice Cream Maker Time: Approximately 25-30 minutes
Makes: 1 ½ quarts
Servings: Ten ½ cup servings

Ingredients:
½ cup coconut flakes
2 tbsp butter
1 cup coconut milk
1/3 cup sugar
2 egg yolks, lightly beaten
2 cups whipping cream
1 teaspoon vanilla

Directions:

1. In a small saucepan, heat coconut flakes and butter over med-low heat.
2. Stir frequently until coconut flakes begin to brown.
3. Remove from heat and cool completely.
4. In another saucepan, stir coconut milk and sugar together.
5. Over medium heat, warm this mixture until it begins to bubble.
6. Beat egg yolks.
7. Pour coconut milk mixture over the egg yolks and whisk to temper the eggs.
8. Pour tempered egg mixture back into the saucepan.
9. Stirring constantly, heat over low-medium heat until it thickens and begins to stick to the back of your spoon.
10. Place in fridge until chilled (about 3 hours).
11. Stir in the whipping cream and vanilla.
12. In ice cream maker, churn about 20-25 minutes or according to manufacturer's instructions.
13. Add cooled toasted coconut to the churning ice cream and churn an additional 5 minutes.

MAPLE WALNUT ICE CREAM RECIPE

Philadelphia Style

Prep Time: 20 minutes
Chill Time: at least 5 hours
Ice Cream Maker Time: Approximately 25-30 minutes
Makes: 1 ½ quarts
Servings: Ten ½ cup servings

Ingredients:
¾ cup maple syrup
1 cup milk
2 cups heavy cream
½ cup chopped walnuts

Directions:

1. Boil maple syrup in a saucepan over medium high heat, for 5 - 10 minutes or until maple syrup has boiled down to about 2/3 cup.
2. Stir milk and cream into hot maple syrup and heat until it just begins to boil.
3. Chill this mixture for at least 5 hours.
4. Pour into ice cream maker.
5. Mix about 20-25 minutes or according to manufacturer's instructions.
6. Add walnuts to ice cream.
7. Mix for 5 more minutes.

MAPLE WALNUT ICE CREAM RECIPE

Custard Style

Prep Time: 25 minutes
Chill Time: at least 5 hours
Ice Cream Maker Time: Approximately 25-30 minutes
Makes: 1 ½ quarts
Servings: Ten ½ cup servings

Ingredients:
¾ cup maple syrup
1 cup milk
2 cups heavy cream
2 eggs
½ cup chopped walnuts

Directions:

1. In a saucepan over medium high heat, boil maple syrup for 5 - 10 minutes or until maple syrup has boiled down to about 2/3 cup.
2. Stir milk and cream into maple syrup and bring to a boil.
3. Beat eggs until they are light and fluffy.
4. Pour hot milk mixture over beaten eggs, mixing well.
5. Pour mixture back into saucepan.
6. Heat. Stir constantly until mixture begins to stick to the back of your spoon and becomes thick. Don't let it boil!
7. Chill for at least 2 hours.
8. Pour into your ice cream maker.
9. Mix about 20-25 minutes or according to manufacturer's instructions.
10. Add walnuts.
11. Continue to mix in ice cream maker for 5 more minutes.

PISTACHIO ICE CREAM RECIPE

Philadelphia Style

Prep Time: 15 minutes
Chill Time: 3 hours
Ice Cream Maker Time: Approximately 20-25 minutes
Makes: 1 ½ quarts
Servings: Ten ½ cup servings

Ingredients:
1 cup shelled pistachios (salted or unsalted)**
¾ cup sugar
1 cup milk
2 cups heavy whipping cream
1 tsp vanilla
¾ cup chopped pistachios (toasted, if desired)

***Helpful Hint:* I shelled my own pistachios for this pistachio ice cream recipe. It was a lot of work! I didn't take the thin peeling off from around the pistachio. As a result, my ice cream was more brown than green. If you want a great color as well as flavor, use shelled pistachios or be sure to take the thin peeling from off the nut.

Directions:

1. Place 1 cup of pistachios and the sugar in your food processor. Process until finely ground. You may have to stir the mixture to make sure that all the nuts have been ground.
2. In a medium saucepan, place ground pistachios and milk.
3. Heat over medium heat, stirring often, until mixture begins to boil.
4. Remove from heat and cool.
5. Place in fridge and chill about 3 hours until mixture is completely cool.
6. Stir in the whipping cream and vanilla.
7. Pour mixture into ice cream maker.
8. Mix about 20-25 minutes or according to manufacturer's instructions.
9. Add chopped pistachios to the churning ice cream.
10. Churn for 5 additional minutes.

PISTACHIO ICE CREAM RECIPE

Custard Style

Prep Time: 15 minutes
Chill Time: at least 3 hours
Ice Cream Maker Time: Approximately 20-25 minutes
Makes: 1 ½ quarts
Servings: Ten ½ cup servings

Ingredients:
2 large eggs
¾ cup sugar
1 cup shelled pistachios (salted or unsalted)**
1 cup milk
2 cups heavy whipping cream
1 tsp vanilla
¾ cup chopped pistachios (toasted, if desired)

**Helpful Hint:* All I had was pistachios in the shell, so I had to shell them myself. Talk about a hand workout! I didn't take the thin peeling off from around the pistachio; so, my ice cream was more brown than green. The texture and flavor were fine though. If you want a great color as well as flavor, use shelled pistachios or be sure to take the thin peeling from off the nut.

Directions:

1. Whisk eggs and ½ cup of sugar in a bowl. Set aside.
2. In a food processor, place 1 cup of pistachios and the remaining ¼ cup sugar. Process until the nuts are ground fine. Note: you might need to stir the mixture to ensure that all the nuts are fully ground.
3. Place ground pistachios and milk in a medium saucepan.
4. Heat over medium heat, stirring often. Bring mixture to a boil.
5. Pour the heated milk mixture over the beaten eggs and whisk together.
6. Pour this mixture back into the saucepan and heat over low heat.
7. Continue to heat until mixture thickens and begins to stick to the back of your spoon.
8. Place in refrigerator and chill about 3 hours until mixture has cooled completely.
9. Stir in the whipping cream and vanilla.
10. Pour mixture into ice cream maker.
11. Churn about 20-25 minutes or according to manufacturer's instructions.
12. Add chopped pistachios to the churning ice cream and churn for 5 more minutes.

VEGAN COCONUT ICE CREAM RECIPE

Philadelphia Style

Prep Time: 15 minutes
Ice Cream Maker Time: Approximately 20-25 minutes

Ingredients:
1 can (15 oz) coconut milk
1/3 cup sugar
1 avocado
2 teaspoon lime juice (or juice from half a lime)

Directions:

1. Stir the sugar and the coconut together until sugar dissolves completely.
2. Mash or puree avocado until it is smooth.
3. Stir avocado into the coconut milk mixture.
4. Add lime juice and combine.
5. Pour this coconut milk mixture into an ice cream maker.
6. Churn about 20-25 minutes or according to manufacturer's instructions.

Just for Fun Recipes

BIRTHDAY CAKE ICE CREAM RECIPE

Philadelphia Style

Prep Time: 12 minutes
Chill Time: at least 3 hours
Ice Cream Maker Time: Approximately 20-25 minutes
Makes: 1 ½ quarts
Servings: Ten ½ cup servings

Ingredients:
1 ½ cups milk
½ cup granulated sugar
2/3 cup cake mix
1 ½ cups heavy whipping cream
1 tsp vanilla extract
1/3 to ½ cup sprinkles

Directions:

1. In a saucepan over medium low heat, combine milk, sugar, and cake mix.
2. Stir constantly until mixture starts to bubble.
3. Remove from heat and cool completely in refrigerator (about 3 hours).
4. Stir in cream and vanilla.
5. Pour into ice cream maker.
6. Mix approximately 15-20 minutes or according to manufacturer's instructions.
7. Add sprinkles to ice cream.
8. Mix in ice cream maker for 5 more minutes.

BIRTHDAY CAKE ICE CREAM RECIPE

Custard Style

Prep Time: 12 minutes
Chill Time: at least 3 hours
Ice Cream Maker Time: Approximately 20-25 minutes
Makes: 1 ½ quarts
Servings: Ten ½ cup servings

Ingredients:
1 ½ cups milk
2/3 cup cake mix
2 eggs
½ cup granulated sugar
1 ½ cups heavy whipping cream
1 tsp vanilla extract
1/3 to ½ cup sprinkles

Directions:

1. In a saucepan over medium low heat, combine milk and cake mix.
2. Stir constantly until mixture starts to bubble.
3. Beat both eggs until they are light and fluffy.
4. Gradually stir in sugar, beating for 1 min.
5. Pour hot cake mixture over eggs, mixing well.
6. Pour mixture back into saucepan and heat over low heat, stirring constantly until mixture thickens and begins to stick to the back of your spoon.
7. Remove from heat and chill in fridge (about 3 hours).
8. Stir in cream and vanilla.
9. Pour into ice cream maker.
10. Mix about 15-20 minutes or according to manufacturer's instructions.
11. Add sprinkles.
12. Mix in ice cream maker for 5 more minutes.

CRÈME BRULEE ICE CREAM RECIPE
Philadelphia Style

Prep Time: 15 minutes
Ice Cream Maker Time: Approximately 20-25 minutes
Makes: 1 ½ quarts
Servings: Ten ½ cup servings

Ingredients:

Caramel/Toffee: 1 cup sugar**

Ice Cream Base

2 eggs
½ cup sugar
1 cup milk

2 cups heavy whipping cream
1 tsp vanilla

**Helpful Hint: Caster sugar will work best for this because it is ground finer (so it melts quicker). However, I made mine with regular granulated sugar (just to make sure it worked). It does! So if that's all you have, you can use granulated sugar. It will just take longer to melt.

Directions:
Caramel/Toffee

1. To make the toffee, line a cookie sheet with aluminum foil.
2. In a small saucepan, place half the sugar (½ cup).
3. Heat over low heat. Stirring frequently, continue to heat sugar until it begins to caramelize. Then add the remaining ½ cup of sugar.
4. When the sugar melts completely, remove from heat and pour over the aluminum lined cookie sheet. Set aside to cool.
5. Once the caramel has cooled completely, remove the foil with the caramel from the cookie sheet and place on a flat work surface.
6. Roll over the hardened caramel with a rolling pin, breaking up the caramel into little pieces – whatever size you desire.
7. Place pieces in a cup, for easy transfer to your ice cream.

Ice Cream Base

1. You can make the ice cream base while the caramel/toffee is cooling.
2. Combine milk with sugar and stir until sugar dissolves completely.
3. Stir in heavy whipping cream and vanilla. Combine.
4. Pour ice cream base into your ice cream machine.
5. Mix about 25-30 minutes or according to manufacturer's instructions.
6. Remove ice cream from ice cream maker and place in a storage container.**
7. Add caramel pieces (including any caramel powder that may have been produced when you broke it up).
8. Stir caramel pieces into ice cream.

**Helpful Hint: Do NOT add caramel pieces to the ice cream maker while it is churning. I broke my caramel pieces up small – about the size of chocolate chips – and tried this. It doesn't work. It's not good for your ice cream maker.

CRÈME BRULEE ICE CREAM RECIPE
Custard Style

Prep Time: 15 minutes
Chill Time: at least 3 hours
Ice Cream Maker Time: Approximately 25-30 minutes
Makes: 1 ½ quarts
Servings: Ten ½ cup servings

Ingredients:
Caramel/Toffee
1 cup sugar**

Ice Cream Base

2 eggs   2 cups heavy whipping cream
½ cup sugar   1 tsp vanilla
1 cup milk

Helpful Hint: Caster sugar is best because it melts quicker (finer grind). I made my toffee with granulated sugar to make sure it would work. It does! So, if you just have granulated sugar, you can use that.

Directions:

Caramel/Toffee

1. First, line a cookie pan with foil.
2. In a small saucepan, place half the sugar (½ cup) and heat over low heat.
3. Heat sugar until it begins to caramelize, stirring often. When sugar begins caramelize, stir in the rest of the sugar (½ cup).
4. When sugar has completely melted, pour it over the foil lined cookie pan.
5. Set aside to cool. Once the caramel has cooled completely, place the foil with the caramel on a countertop (remove from pan).
6. With a rolling pin, roll over the hardened caramel to break the caramel into little pieces (large or small) I prefer smaller pieces.
7. Transfer to a small container so you can easily add them to your ice cream.

Ice Cream Base

1. Make the ice cream base while the caramel/toffee is cooling.
2. Whisk eggs and sugar together in a bowl. Set aside.
3. In a saucepan, heat milk over medium heat until it just begins to boil.
4. Pour heated milk over the beaten egg and sugar mixture. Whisk together.
5. Pour mixture back into the saucepan and heat over low heat.
6. Heat until it thickens and begins to stick to the back of your spoon.
7. Place in fridge and chill about 3 hours until mixture has cooled completely.
8. Once cool, stir in heavy whipping cream and vanilla. Combine well.
9. Pour this ice cream base into your ice cream machine.
10. Churn about 25-30 minutes or according to manufacturer's instructions.
11. Remove ice cream from ice cream maker and place in a storage container.**
12. Add caramel pieces (including any caramel powder). Stir into ice cream.

Helpful Hint: Do NOT add caramel pieces to the ice cream maker while it is churning. I broke my caramel pieces up small (about the size of chocolate chips) and tried this. It doesn't work. It's not good for your maker.

EGG NOG ICE CREAM RECIPE

Philadelphia Style

Prep Time: 10 minutes
Ice Cream Maker Time: Approximately 25-30 minutes
Makes: 1 ½ quarts
Servings: Ten ½ cup servings

Ingredients:
½ cup pasteurized egg products (Egg Beaters)
¾ cup granulated sugar
1 cup milk
2 cups whipping cream
1 tsp imitation rum extract
½ tsp vanilla extract
¼ tsp nutmeg

Directions:

1. Place egg product and sugar in a bowl. Beat with an electric mixer on medium speed about 1 ½ to 2 minutes until pale yellow and thick.
2. Stir in milk, whipping cream, extracts, and nutmeg, blending well.
3. Pour the ice cream base into your ice cream maker.
4. Mix in ice cream maker about 25-30 minutes or according to manufacturer's instructions.

EGG NOG ICE CREAM RECIPE

Custard Style

Prep Time: 25 minutes
Chill Time: 3 hours
Ice Cream Maker Time: Approximately 25-30 minutes
Makes: 1 ½ quarts
Servings: Ten ½ cup servings

Ingredients:
4 egg yolks
¾ cup granulated sugar
1 cup milk
1 tsp imitation rum extract
½ tsp vanilla extract
¼ tsp nutmeg
2 cups whipping cream

Directions:

1. Place eggs and sugar in a small bowl and beat well until light and fluffy.
2. In a medium saucepan, heat milk until it just starts to bubble.
3. Pour the hot milk over the beaten egg mixture and then stir well.
4. Pour milk/egg mixture back into saucepan and heat. Stir constantly until mixture becomes thick and begins to stick to the back of a spoon.
5. Chill for at least 3 hours.
6. After mixture has chilled, stir in rum and vanilla extracts and nutmeg. Stir in whipping cream.
7. Pour the egg nog ice cream base into your ice cream maker.
8. Mix for 25-30 minutes (or according to manufacturer's instructions).

GINGERBREAD ICE CREAM RECIPE

Philadelphia Style

Prep Time: 10 minutes
Ice Cream Maker Time: Approximately 25-30 minutes
Makes: 1 ½ quarts
Servings: Ten ½ cup servings

Ingredients:
1 cup milk
1/3 cup brown sugar
2 tbsp molasses
1 tsp ground cinnamon
¼ tsp nutmeg
¼ tsp ground cloves
2 cups whipping cream

Directions:

1. Whisk milk and sugar together to completely dissolve the sugar.
2. Stir in molasses, cinnamon, nutmeg, and cloves.
3. Add heavy whipping cream and blend well.
4. Pour into your ice cream maker.
5. Churn in ice cream maker about 25-30 minutes or according to manufacturer's instructions.

Helpful Hint: If you want a hint of gingerbread flavor, rather than a strong flavor, just reduce the amount of spices you add to the ice cream mixture.

GINGERBREAD ICE CREAM RECIPE

Custard Style

Prep Time: 25 minutes
Chill Time: 3 hours
Ice Cream Maker Time: Approximately 25-30 minutes
Makes: 1 ½ quarts
Servings: Ten ½ cup servings

Ingredients:
3 egg yolks
1 cup milk
1/3 cup brown sugar
2 tbsp molasses
1 tsp ground cinnamon
¼ tsp nutmeg
¼ tsp ground cloves
2 cups whipping cream

Directions:

1. Place eggs in a small bowl and beat well. Set aside
2. In a saucepan, mix milk, brown sugar, molasses, cinnamon, nutmeg, and cloves. Heat until it just starts to bubble.
3. Pour hot milk mixture over beaten egg mixture. Stir well.
4. Pour this mixture back into saucepan and heat, stirring constantly until mixture becomes thick and sticks to the back of a spoon.
5. Chill for at least 3 hours.
6. After mixture has chilled, stir in heavy whipping cream.
7. Pour into your ice cream machine.
8. Mix for 25-30 minutes (or according to manufacturer's instructions).

Helpful Hint: If you want a hint of gingerbread flavor, rather than a strong flavor, just reduce the amount of spices you add to the ice cream mixture.

GINGERBREAD COOKIE ICE CREAM RECIPE

Philadelphia Style

Prep Time: 10 minutes
Ice Cream Maker Time: Approximately 25-30 minutes
Makes: 1 ½ quarts
Servings: Ten ½ cup servings

Ingredients:
1 cup milk
½ cup sugar
2 cups whipping cream
1 ½ tsp vanilla extract
¾ cup crushed gingerbread cookies (or gingersnaps)*
*Place gingerbread cookies in a Ziploc bag. Seal bag and crush cookies with the heel of your hand.

Directions:

1. Whisk milk and sugar together to completely dissolve the sugar.
2. Stir in heavy whipping cream and vanilla.
3. Pour into your ice cream maker.
4. Churn in ice cream maker about 20-25 minutes or according to manufacturer's instructions.
5. Add crushed gingerbread cookies to the churning mixture.
6. Churn for 5 more minutes.

GINGERBREAD COOKIE ICE CREAM RECIPE

Custard Style

Prep Time: 25 minutes
Chill Time: 2 hours
Ice Cream Maker Time: Approximately 25-30 minutes
Makes: 1 ½ quarts
Servings: Ten ½ cup servings

Ingredients:
2 eggs
½ cup granulated sugar
1 cup milk
2 cups whipping cream
1 ½ tsp vanilla extract
¾ cup crushed gingerbread cookies (or ginger snaps)

Directions:

1. Place eggs and sugar in a small bowl and beat until light and fluffy. Set aside.
2. In a saucepan, heat milk until it just starts to bubble.
3. Pour hot milk over beaten egg mixture. Stir well.
4. Pour this mixture back into saucepan and heat, stirring constantly until mixture becomes thick and sticks to the back of a spoon.
5. Chill for at least 3 hours.
6. After mixture has chilled, stir in heavy whipping cream and vanilla.
7. Pour into your ice cream machine.
8. Mix for 20-25 minutes (or according to manufacturer's instructions).
9. Add crushed cookies to the churning mixture.
10. Churn an additional 5 minutes.

PUDDING ICE CREAM RECIPE

Philadelphia Style

Prep Time: 8 minutes
Ice Cream Maker Time: Approximately 25-30 minutes
Makes: 1 ½ quarts
Servings: Ten ½ cup servings

Ingredients:
1 package (3.5 or 4 oz) instant pudding mix – the flavor of your choice
¼ cup sugar
1 cup milk
2 cups heavy whipping cream

Directions:

1. Mix pudding mix with sugar and combine well.
2. Add whipping cream and stir.
3. Pour into your ice cream machine and let it do the rest of the work.
4. Churn about 25-30 minutes or according to manufacturer's instructions.

Yup! Pudding ice cream is really that easy.

PUDDING ICE CREAM RECIPE

Custard Style

Prep Time: 15 minutes
Chill Time: at least 3 hours
Ice Cream Maker Time: Approximately 25-30 minutes
Makes: 1 ½ quarts
Servings: Ten ½ cup servings

Ingredients:
2 eggs
1/8 cup sugar
1 cup milk
2 cups heavy whipping cream
1 package (3.5 or 4 oz) instant pudding mix – the flavor of your choice

Directions:

1. With a whisk, beat eggs and sugar together until smooth.
2. In a saucepan, heat milk over medium heat until bubbles begin to form on top of the milk.
3. Pour the hot milk over the beaten eggs and lightly whisk together.
4. Pour this egg and milk mixture back into the saucepan.
5. Continue to heat over medium heat until the mixture thickens and begins to stick to the back of your spoon.
6. Chill completely. This will take at least 3 hours.
7. Once milk has chilled, add whipping cream and combine.
8. Stir in pudding mix, combining well.
9. Pour mixture into your ice cream maker.
10. Allow this to churn for 25-30 minutes or according to manufacturer's instructions.

SNOW ICE CREAM RECIPE

Philadelphia Style

Ingredients:
1 cup milk
½ teaspoon vanilla
½ cup sugar
4 - 5 cups unpacked snow
Food coloring
Ice cream cones or serving bowls

Directions:

1. Mix milk, vanilla, and sugar together in a large bowl until the sugar completely dissolves.
2. Gather some clean, newly fallen snow.
3. Stir the snow and the milk mixture together. Stir constantly until it the mixture looks like ice cream.

Flavor Variations:

1. Colored Ice Cream that looks like Sno Cones: Stir in a few drops of food coloring!
2. Hot Chocolate Flavored Ice Cream: Instead of the vanilla, stir in 2 tbsp of cooled hot chocolate!
3. Coffee Flavored Ice Cream: Instead of vanilla, stir in 2 tbsp of your favorite coffee (cooled)!
4. Ice Cream with Mix-Ins: Stir some of your favorite mix-ins into the ice cream (chocolate chips, cookie crumbs, etc.)!

RECIPE INDEX

Looking for more great ice cream recipes?
Want some great ice cream resources?

Check out...

SERVING-ICE-CREAM.COM
the art of making, serving, and selling ice cream

We'll see you there!

Made in the USA
Las Vegas, NV
10 December 2020

12640809R00069